The Smuggler: No Gentleman

Smuggling with violence around Christchurch and Poole Bays

M. A. Hodges MA

ISBN 1 897 887 20 5

A British Library Cataloguing in Publication Data.
A catalogue record for this book is available from the British Library.

Published by: Natula Publications
5 St. Margaret's Avenue, Christchurch, Dorset BH23 1JD

Cover illustration: Part of a 1539 map showing Christchurch and Poole Bays including Christchurch Harbour and Bourne Stream, by kind permission of Arthur Lloyd.

THE SMUGGLER: NO GENTLEMAN

Smuggling with violence around Christchurch and Poole Bays

"Them that asks no question in't told a lie -
Watch the wall my darling, while the Gentlemen go by."
(Kipling - *Puck of Pooks Hill*)

When the Owlers are out, you needn't ask for why,
Cross those Gentlemen my darling and you will surely die.
(with apologies to Kipling)

A great deal of nonsense has been written about the 'romance' of smuggling, as if smugglers were pursuing some sort of amusing sport or hobby. Smugglers were criminals engaging in a reign of terror, prepared to use torture, kidnapping and murder in the furtherance of greed. By these means, they took advantage of the poor exploiting their labour and exposing them to the risks of imprisonment, transportation, impressment into the Navy or even death on the gallows.

Eventually, by the mid-eighteenth century, smugglers had won control over large areas and, as with the Sicilian Mafia, they were condoned by the local gentry, who were frequently involved not only as customers but also, sometimes, as financiers of 'the trade'. The smuggler often enjoyed the support of the society in which he operated, which included magistrates, jurymen, clergy and the gentry. However, the smuggling gangs were brutal and violent people, prepared to maim or kill. They also used terrorism and bribery. Their operations would extend from housebreaking to highway robbery, wrecking and piracy. With their numbers far in excess of local revenue men, gangs could operate as small armies and were able to engage in pitched battle with the Revenue, even when the latter was supported by military and naval forces. At one time about a quarter of all trade conducted was in smuggled or contraband goods, this had obvious consequences for the Exchequer and lawful commerce.

Any State requires revenue to maintain itself and to protect its citizens. A tax on the movement of goods, often in kind, was an early and obvious way of raising revenue. It has always been customary, hence customs. Evasion of the customary tax, known as a duty when crossing a boundary, is called smuggling. The name comes from the Anglo-Saxon word smugan 'to creep', i.e. stealthy. The official name for smuggling, in the early days, was fraud.

Fraud in the Christchurch area had a long history, from pre-Romans times, when the Celts at Hengistbury Head were forging coins by dipping bronze in silver. The inhabitants of Hengistbury (Christchurch) were importing wine from the Mediterranean before the Romans came. This also occurred at Green Island and Hamworthy on Poole Harbour and possibly Ampress at Lymington. After the Roman invasion, the Roman fleet based at Bitterne (Clausentum) on the Itchen enforced custom duties - the portoria - for the Emperors. The Recreation Ground in Christchurch is part of the original Portfield, a name derived from the town being a market, and originating from the Roman word.

The first record of an actual customs duty dates from 743. A Mercian Charter refers to dues on ships at London. By 979 records list dues on wood, wine, cloth, fish and dairy products. It was usual for 'petty customs' to be charged on goods brought to market in a town. These were levied for the benefit of the town or manor, often with local residents exempt. The first charter for Christchurch c.1140 was of this type. Duty could be raised on exports as well as imports. The Winchester Assize of 1203 placed one fifteenth duty on all imports and exports, to be reported to the Treasury and not through the local sheriffs and lords. The duty was to be gathered by a Collector with a separate Comptroller to keep accounts. A 'New Custom' of half a mark (6/8d = 33p) a bag of wool was introduced in 1275. It was successful and was so increased in 1298 on each 364lb bale exported. Even today, the Lord Chancellor in the House of Lords sits on the Woolsack. The wool tax was 'farmed' out to contractors who bid for the annual right to collect duties at specific ports. The export of wool was temporarily banned in 1337 in order to protect local cloth manufacture (a cottage industry at that time), and to damage the foreign manufacturers. The wool export smugglers were known as 'owlers', perhaps because they worked at night or their name may be a derivation of 'wooler'. Also at that time spherical clay containers, as made at Verwood, with two lugs like owl's eyes were used by farm labourers and fishermen to carry the day's cider ration. These were called owls and would have been used by owlers.

In 1353 certain ports were designated as 'staples', where wool was weighed for taxation by Kings Beams (scales), as still exist outside the former Custom House at Poole. Perhaps Staple Cross near Burton, outside Christchurch, was used for this purpose. Other staples were designated for bulk goods such as tin, lead and grain. Poole became a port of the staple for Dorset in 1453, replacing Melcombe Regis (Weymouth). Up to 1531 Southampton was a staple for metals including Cornish tin. Foreign trade was only lawful from an approved port or place (as is still the case). By 1559 Southampton was still the only 'staple' for the County of Hampshire. Collectors of Customs were based at ports of the staple.

In the early seventeenth century all England and Wales was included in a Great Farm on a centralised system. It was only in 1671 that Customs Commissioners were appointed by the Crown. In 1643 Excise Tax was introduced, as a Civil War measure; like Income Tax in 1799 in the war against Napoleon and the 1940 Purchase Tax (now VAT) in the Second World War. Effective temporary taxes like these soon became permanent. The Excise was farmed until 1683 when Excise Commissioners were appointed. The Customs and Excise were not combined until 1909. (The author was an Officer of Customs and Excise in the 1960s, when 4,000 such officers were responsible for gathering half the nation's revenue while only 70 of us were in the Investigation Branch). The European Common Market, VAT and decimalisation caused a major Customs and Excise reorganisation in 1972. The Commission of an Officer of Customs and Excise (in the 1960s) empowered him to call out the armed forces and police, to break into property and even open fire, but weapons were not issued!

Besides the violence associated with smuggling, coastal places were also at risk from pirates and raids from foreign powers. Vespasian's attack on Wessex in 46AD included Roman navy units and a supply base at Hamworthy in Poole Harbour. Also usurpers like Carausius, who may have been at Clausentum in 286, would have produced a similar effect. The reconquest in 296 may have involved a landing at Christchurch Harbour as part of a two-pronged attack also made on Kent. The withdrawal of the fleet from Bitterne by 410 and the destruction of the last British field army in about 540, after the successful resistance by Arthur, further increased the risk of raids. Saxons arrived in Christchurch Harbour: Cerdic and Cynric with five ships at Cerdic's Ora in 495 and in 514 they were followed by Stuff and Whitgar with three ships. Cerdic and Cynric took the Isle of Wight from the Jutes in 530. Although many Britons went to live in Amorcia (Brittany), the delay in the Saxon conquest caused by Arthur gave time for some of the pagan invaders to become Christian and so to coexist with Britons in what was to become Wessex.

Viking raids began in 787 when three long ships from Norway, via Ireland, arrived at Weymouth. The reeve, Beaduheard, rode down from Dorchester to levy any customs duty for the King but the Vikings killed him. This is the first record of an officer murdered in the exercise of his duty.

Royal Navy and Smugglers Hand to Hand c. 1820
By kind permission of Mark Bullen, Wrington, Somerset.

Local assaults were no doubt common after the breakdown of Roman law and order and the destruction of the 'Saxon Shore' coast system which included forts at Portchester, Carisbrooke and Corfe and a signal station on St. Catherine's Hill (Christchurch). Attacks on coastal towns like Wareham, Poole, Lymington, Yarmouth, Portsmouth and Southampton would often place Twynham (Christchurch) at the risk of attack. Other raids followed:

789	Wareham and Poole attacked by three ships.
837	Hamwic, on the west bank of the Itchen, attacked by 33 ships which were driven off. The 33 ships went to Portland which they attacked successfully.
838	Hamwic again attacked; this time the settlement was burnt.
860	Portchester raided. Hamton, south-west of Hamwic, on the south-east bank of the Test attacked. This enclosed settlement became known as South-Hampton to distinguish it from Hamwic. Winchester also attacked.
871	Wareham, the local monastery destroyed. Attacks on Wareham up the Frome went past the site of Poole which must have been open to attack.
876	Wareham, where Alfred blockaded the Danes who escaped by land to Exeter. Their fleet of 120 ships put out into Poole Bay while under attack. A gale from the north-east drove them ashore in Studland and Swanage Bays as wrecks, early in 877.
877	Alfred built large warships and so defeated the Danes at sea.
897	Isle of Wight attacked by six ships: only one escaped.
980	Southampton attacked by seven ships which captured people as slaves.
981	Portland attacked by three ships.
984	Southampton raided.
994	Weymouth and Wareham both raided. Poole and Christchurch possibly attacked. The Danes over-wintered at Southampton.
998	Isle of Wight raided.
999	Isle of Wight (The pirates over-wintered on the Medina).
1000	Isle of Wight raided.
1006	Isle of Wight raided.

1009	Southampton raided.
1010	Southampton raided.
1011	Isle of Wight raided.
1012	Isle of Wight raided.
1013	Southampton raided. Probably about this time the wall of the Burgh at Christchurch was strengthened by ironstone from Hengistbury Head.
1014	Southampton raided.
1015	Brownsea, used as a store by Canute for his plunder from Cerne Abbey.
1016	Wareham raided. Canute became King when he was elected at Southampton.
1047	Isle of Wight raided.

The above schedule is no doubt incomplete, but it serves to show the dangers faced by the inhabitants of the shores of Hampshire and Dorset.

The Normans maintained the arrangement of levying local customs duties moving into or out of a Borough. The Normans built castles to control the coast at: Portchester, Carisbrooke, Southampton, Christchurch, Wareham Corfe and Portland. These were all involved in The Anarchy, when Matilda, daughter of Henry I, was at war with Stephen, her cousin, who landed at Southampton in 1136 to claim the throne. The following year he sacked Wareham and in 1137 and 1139 besieged Corfe which was held by de Redvers who also held Plymton, Exeter, Christchurch and Carisbrooke Castles. In 1142 Wareham was again burnt and Robert of Gloucester landed in Poole to support Matilda. In 1147 Henry, Matilda's son, landed at Wareham, where his troops promptly plundered the monastery. The sacking of Wareham by Stephen and the damage done by Gloucester's troops probably aided the development of Poole. Henry II succeeded to the throne in 1154 when he landed at Lepe. Christchurch received a Charter from de Redvers in about 1140 in exchange for the responsibility of town defence, but although Poole's ships are mentioned in 1170 it did not receive a charter until a century or so later, perhaps in 1248, when William Longspee needed money for a crusade.

Christchurch Castle and Constables Hall
Engraving of a drawing, S. Hooper, 1783.

Ships for the Crusades sailed from Southampton to join the fleet at Dartmouth, in 1194 Richard I gathered his fleet at Portsmouth to attack the French. From 1204-1220 the French threatened invasion. They had troops in England in about 1213 when the Dauphin built a wooden castle near Aldborne in Wiltshire. In 1206 Christchurch, Yarmouth and Keyhaven were ordered to provide ships for the King. Impressment into the navy is reported in 1208. In 1224, 1229 and 1230 Poole was ordered to provide shipping. In 1230 the fleet was again assembled at Portsmouth, and once more in 1242 when the French attempted a blockade. Southampton was ordered to send two ships to the Channel Isles to put down piracy in 1241. In 1254 Poole was ordered to provide ships large enough to carry 16 horses.

In 1290 the Bailiff of Poole was ordered to levy four shillings a tun on each tun of wine (i.e. two pipes or four hogsheads) from Bergerac and St. Emilion. The King also took prisage, which was one tun (large cask) in every 10 to 19 landed, and two tuns in every 20 or over. This tax was abolished in 1308 and replaced by a duty of two shillings on every tun.

Pirates based on the Cinque Ports of Kent and Sussex destroyed much of Portsmouth in 1294. The Cinque Ports were jealous of their special privileges from the Crown and resisted the growth of other ports. The following year Poole supplied three ships for the King. In 1297 seven ships from Southampton and one each from Christchurch, Lymington and Beaulieu, and others from Poole were taken up to carry military supplies to Gascony. The rents of Christchurch fell in 1298, perhaps due to fire, plague or plunder. In 1300 a duty of two pence was levied on each person travelling abroad. In 1302 ports were ordered to supply ships for the Scots War: Southampton supplied two, Poole, Wareham and Brownsea two each, Weymouth one and the Prior of Christchurch one. Shipping was again requisitioned from Christchurch, Lymington and Yarmouth in the following year.

In 1303 Genoese galleys came to trade at Southampton. Venetian and Florentine vessels followed them in later years and an Italian quarter developed in the town. Spanish vessels also visited the area and in 1305 one such vessel ran ashore at Portland and was plundered. A total of 235 locals were charged with plunder of the vessel. The following year a vessel loaded with wine was also plundered when wrecked near Swanage.

The Scots War resulted in further calls for shipping. In 1311 three were asked of Southampton and a total of three from Poole and Lymington. It appears that Christchurch had by then become too poor or too shallow to provide ships for the Crown. Venetian galleys called at Southampton, in 1319, to trade. As a result there was a skirmish and some of their crews were killed. Local people continued to be violent. In 1321 men from Lymington plundered a Portuguese vessel off the Isle of Wight.

At the same time the men of the Cinque Ports had a private war with Poole, Lyme Regis and Weymouth, and 30 ships from Winchelsea attacked vessels at Southampton burning 17 ships. The Crown largely relied on the Cinque Ports to provide a Royal Navy when required: the privileges of these ports gave them a degree of immunity from punishment.

In 1322 Poole provided the King with four ships but Southampton provided only two. Two years later Keyhaven, Boldre and Lymington provided two ships, as did Poole, to aid the Crown in its war with Scotland. It was usual for Scotland and France to act together to divide the English forces and prevent the English King from bringing all his power to bear on one enemy at a time. In 1326 ships above 50 tons were ordered to join the Western Fleet at Portsmouth. During the following year the French attacked Southampton and Portsmouth.

The father of Geoffrey Chaucer (himself a Customs Comptroller at London between 1374 and 1386) was the Customs Collector at Southampton. It was already evident that corruption was common. In 1328 men of Lymington were charged with avoiding customs duties and at Southampton in 1333 customs weighers of wool were dismissed for lack of diligence.

The Hundred Years War, a period of intermittent conflict between the years 1336 and 1453 saw the coast on both sides of the Channel open to attack. There was great destruction on both sides: -

1336	French vessels entered the Solent and sank and captured shipping.
1337	French off the Isle of Wight were intending to invade. Portland, Melcombe Regis, Wareham, Poole and Lymington burnt.
1338	French attacked Portsmouth with 50 ships, town burnt.

1339 French, with Genoese and Catalan (Spanish) support, devastated Southampton which had no walls on its seaward side at the time. The townsfolk were caught in church on a Sunday morning; a massacre took place and women were raped in the church. The town rallied and a leader of the attack, a son of the King of Sicily (a Norman) was killed with some 200 of his men. In the same year ships from Southampton and Poole attacked, as pirates, the ships belonging to their own King's brother.

1341 The Black Death entered Britain through Melcombe Regis.

1342 Portsmouth burnt. Poole provided ships to support John de Montfort in France.

1345 Southampton provided five ships for the King's attack on France. (Three customs officers were fined and dismissed at Southampton).

1346 Southampton provided 21 ships for King Edward III, also, Hamble provided 7, Isle of Wight 13, Lymington 9 and Portsmouth 5, en-route to the victory at Crécy. The associated naval attack destroyed over 100 French vessels.

1347 Poole had four ships at the siege of Calais.
Tunnage and Poundage was introduced: 2/- a ton (tun) on wine and 6d in the £ on other imports.

1354 Lymington men again charged with avoiding customs dues since Southampton claimed Lymington was within its port.

1364 Winchelsea, one of the Cinque Ports, confirmed the boundaries of Poole Harbour.

1365 First mention of guns for coastal defence at Quarr Abbey, Isle of Wight. Poole made a magazine and garrison.

1370 Portsmouth sacked; Isle of Wight attacked and Lymington and Poole burnt. Perhaps Christchurch was too small to attack or, more likely, the existence of the castle in the town saved it.

1371 A ship from Dartmouth plundered at Kimmeridge by local people.

Calshot Castle
Engraving of a painting by W.H. Bartlett, 1820.

ransom. In 1631 there was a payment of one shilling for seven men taken by Dunkirk pirates. Poole again complained of Turks upon the coasts in 1636 and in 1638 Algiers pirates were off Poole Harbour. The following year an English ship was taken off the Isle of Wight by eight 'Turkish' vessels, and the crew sold as slaves in Algiers. In 1647 six European officers on a Sallee rover mutinied and brought their vessel into Southampton.

Piracy was also a local occupation. Traders turned privateer and privateer turned pirate as opportunity offered. In 1577 and 1593 local pirates were active off Poole. Commissioners for the suppression of piracy were appointed in 1578 and 1585. Some pirates had powerful protectors, like the courtier Sir Christopher Hatton, who protected Heynes the pirate. Francis Hawley the Vice Admiral of Dorset at Corfe Castle wrote in 1582 to Secretary of State Walsingham complaining of the so numerous pirates operating in the area, that 'in truth they are my master'. A Customs Searcher testified that year that Heynes had three tons of Brazil wood stored in the chapel at Brownsea and 112 hogsheads of Scottish herrings in the castle there. In 1586 the Keeper of Brownsea Castle bought goods from pirates: 40 bags of raisins and two bags of almonds, in exchange for cash and a boatload of bread and beer to victual their vessel. At one time a pirate shanty town existed at Lulworth; it was removed in favour of Studland.

Hurst Castle was also involved in smuggling at an early date. In 1572 three hogsheads of wine were brought to Hurst from the Isle of Wight for local sale. Such behaviour continued, in 1629 the Lieutenant of Hurst Castle was found to be keeping smuggled tobacco there.

A map of 1587 shows what appears to be a three gun battery on Hengistbury Head with others at Taddiford, Friar's Cliff (later Steamer Point) and Lansdowne. No doubt such emergency beach batteries were in case of attack by the Spanish Armada in 1588. (Hengistbury, Mudeford, Brownsea and Swanage had emergency beach batteries in 1940-44). Active defences against the Armada included Henry VIII artillery castles as at Hurst and Brownsea, also possibly forts (sconces) at Poole and Hamworthy, and the medieval castle at Corfe. The block house to guard the landing at Bournemouth was still in use. There were coastal beacons at Hengistbury, Lansdowne and Canford Cliffs. They were manned by sentries known as 'hoblars' meaning light horsemen who hobbled their horses while on watch.

The captains of artillery castles at Brownsea and Calshot were capable of using their guns to exact private dues from passing vessels. In February 1589 the Keeper of Brownsea fired on the *Bountiful Gift* when it sought to leave the harbour, even though it had a licence from Poole, because it had no pass from the Vice Admiral at Corfe. The captain and one of the crew of the ship were killed and so the Keeper was charged with murder by the coroner's jury. He was condemned to death at Corfe but released in December 1590.

In later Tudor times Studland Bay, west of Poole Bay, which as with Christchurch Bay enjoys double tides, was a popular resort for pirate vessels which were able to lie in shelter but able to dash out and snatch up shipping in the Channel. A well-known pirate, Robert Reneger, who captured a Spanish treasure ship, was made the Customs Surveyor at Southampton in the reign of Edward VI. Another local pirate, John Piers, was hung at Studland in 1582; the pirates later cut down the gallows and threatened to burn Poole. His contemporary pirate Stephen Heynes was lost at sea. Such men were greatly feared for their dreadful cruelties. The crews of captured vessels were usually sent 'home by sea' i.e. thrown overboard. Such an end was merciful compared to what Heynes would do. His practice was to disembowel his victims and nail their entrails to the mast, then make them dance around to wind their guts around the mast. (A pagan rite used to make victims acknowledge a totem pole). Such activities gave rise to the couplet: 'If Poole was a fish pool and the men of Poole fish, there'd be a pool for the devil and a fish for his dish'.

Dunkirk was a particular base for pirates. In 1600 they were so much a threat that vessels refused to sail from Poole for Ireland. In 1628 it was reported that three or four Dunkirkers could be seen every day from Purbeck cliffs.

The chances of wind and weather in the Channel and on the coasts, coupled with the risks from war and pirates, bred up experience and a ruthless attitude amongst seafarers of the English Channel. A few non-uniformed and sparsely armed revenue men working for merchants who farmed the revenue would not overawe seamen who wished to engage in smuggling.

Any wrecked vessel, i.e. abandoned and hull touching the bottom, became the property of the Crown, subject to local variations. Usually the local Lord of the Manor was entitled to a share. In Christchurch the Monks at the Priory had a Tythe of Wreck. The Customs Collectors were to become the Receivers of Wreck for the Crown, (now the local Officer of Customs and Excise has this duty). Goods which floated off a vessel at sea and which were picked up at sea were flotsam; goods jettisoned, for example to lighten a vessel in distress, were jetsam; such flotsam and jetsam became a responsibility of the Admiralty.

West Cowes Castle
Engraving of drawing by Roberts, c.1790.

In late medieval times much of England's international trade was in the hands of 'Italian' merchants. Genoese and Venetian merchants smuggled goods in and out of Southampton in the fifteenth century. The growing risks run by revenue men are demonstrated by the injuries inflicted on a Customs Searcher at Poole in 1453, who was stabbed in the face, through the nose and into the mouth. Also by the riot at Lyme Regis in 1576 when customs men sought to search shipping to prevent bullion export smuggling. In 1588 the coasts stood ready to resist the Spanish Armada as it sailed up the Channel past the Isle of Wight. Ships from Portsmouth, Southampton and Poole were in the English fleet and were in action off Portland and Wight. They were supported by smaller supply vessels from other local ports. The *San Salvador*, a captured Armada flagship, blew up and sank off Handfast Point (Old Harry Rocks).

The Protestants at La Rochelle were sent aid by the Stuart government in 1626. Poole ships were involved in that year and in 1627. The expedition was a disastrous failure.

Southampton and Poole had become great rivals. In medieval times Southampton had shared the wine trade with Bristol, but from Tudor times Poole had developed trade with Newfoundland. Poole ships would sail to the Grand Banks to catch cod, dry and salt the fish on shore and then carry it to Spain and other Mediterranean coasts, returning home with wine, dried fruit, olives and other exotic products. It was not uncommon for the mariners from different English ports to be virtually at war with one another.

During the Civil War many new Excise duties were introduced or increased: wine, beer, cider, coffee, chocolate, sherbet, cordials and tea. Similarly customs duties were increased on goods such as wine, brandy, rum, gin, tea, cocoa beans, coffee beans, tobacco, snuff, pepper and lace. In 1660 it was again forbidden to export wool to prevent English manufacturers being undercut by cheaper foreign labour. A proclamation was made against 'Smuckellors' in 1661. The smugglers' names for the revenue men varied (many are unprintable). Common names were Philistines or Landsharks.

Christchurch made its last payment of the Ship Money Tax in 1639 and the Civil War soon followed. The Civil War and Republican Commonwealth was a time of social disruption. Wareham had been Royalist. It changed hands several times amid scenes of rape and murder. Poole was Parliamentarian and successfully resisted attempts at its capture. Christchurch had started as Royalist but had been captured without a fight and then held by Parliament against attempts at recapture which included a three day siege of the Castle and Priory. Southampton and Lymington were for Parliament and so was Portsmouth after ejecting its original Royalist Governor. Lyme Regis withstood a six week close siege as a Parliamentarian stronghold. Corfe Castle was held for the King by gallant Lady Bankes. Generally ports and manufacturing towns were for Parliament while the conservative rural areas and their landowners were for the King.

An inscription dating from these times is on a tomb at Christchurch Priory, for Henry Rogers of Hoburne, who died in 1641.

'We were not slain but raised
Raised not to life
But to be buried twice
By men of strife
What rest could living have
When dead had none
Agree amongst you
Here we ten are one.'

The verse may refer to bodies, perhaps drowned men buried possibly urgently on a beach, later dug up for burial in a Christian churchyard. However, it may instead refer to old lead coffins being dug up in the Priory area for the metal to be cast into bullets. The ten skeletons concerned, perhaps former monks, being reinterred in one convenient tomb.

After the Restoration of the Monarchy in 1660 returning royalist supporters were faced with parliamentarian supporters in ownership of sequested estates purchased from the Government. The Puritans found their clergy, who had taken over Church of England livings, put out, and the former royalist clergy reinstalled, as happened at Christchurch. The old parliamentary supporters were concerned about the return of the Court and its favourites and debauched lifestyles. Many people with naval and military skills were out of work. Such men made good smugglers as governments were to discover time and time again. Luxury goods like tea could cost 15 shillings an ounce duty paid in 1657, so there was a real incentive to smuggle.

There was little in the way of a welfare system. The Poor Laws of Elizabeth I were still in force against 'study beggars'. The 1662 Law of Settlement had laid down that the destitute could only get relief in their own parish, usually that of their birth. This could mean that widows had to return to their birth parish where they may no longer have family or friends. Pregnant pauper women would be given passage money to return to their parish of origin to avoid their baby becoming a burden on their present place of residence. The Game Laws were in force against poaching. There were no pensions for elderly people or ex-servicemen. The disabled were usually left to beg, or to claim charity. The individual relied on their family for support. Those without a family were destitute if they had no savings or property. Later the Combination Acts were passed to stop men banding together to achieve higher wages.

In 1655 representations were made to Cromwell to open the Avon to vessels of 30 tons burden drawing three feet of water. It is known that in 1625 John Taylor and five men took a wherry up the Avon from Christchurch to Crane Bridge, Salisbury. The River Avon Navigation Act was passed in 1664 (it is still on the statute book) to improve the water route from Christchurch to Crane Bridge near Fisherton Street in Salisbury. Vessels of 25 tons burden were making this journey until at least the first third of the eighteenth century. This would be an improved route to a good market for smugglers. This Act may have been the cause of building at Mudeford Quay, there was an Inn there by 1699. This quay became the site of a Dutch Colony, possibly religious refugees. It was reported of the smugglers in 1677 ' ... owlers a militia that in defiance of all authority convey their wool to shallops with such strength that officers dare not offend them'. It is possible that wool was exported from Mudeford Haven since it is on the direct route from Staple Cross, just east of Christchurch, outside the tax jurisdiction of the Medieval Priory.

In 1679 it was reported that the coast from Poole to Lymington was full of landing places where 'vast quantities of French goods were landed'. The following year saw riots at Lymington, Pennington and Milford and wine was seized at Hurst.

The 1664 Act meant that in 1675 Salisbury was envisaged as a potential sea port. That year the Bishop of Salisbury made the first cut for the improved waterway. Also in 1675 Andrew Yarrenton surveyed the Avon and emphasised the development potential of Christchurch Harbour. He published 'England's Improvements by Sea and Land' in 1677 which recommended the development of Christchurch Harbour as a naval base, with a fort at Hengistbury and an iron foundry at Ringwood. The navigation to Salisbury from Christchurch was in use by 1682 since two vessels were recorded at Crane Bridge that year, each with 25 tons of cargo. There is a record of the navigation being inspected in 1692. Although the navigation of the Avon was damaged by floods, Daniel Defoe recorded in 1727 that it was in use to within two miles of Salisbury.

Hurst Castle
Engraving of a drawing by W.H.Bartlett, c 1830

In 1693 the Earl of Clarendon had a new entrance made into Christchurch Harbour through the Mudeford Spit. An ironstone breakwater was built on the south-east side of the new entrance, this is shown on a map of 1698. In 1697-8 an Admiralty report stated that Christchurch Harbour was useful for vessels under 30 tons burden. However, Clarendon's new entrance was damaged by a storm in 1730 and disappeared by 1916. A few stones remain visible at low tide, known today as the Clarendon Rocks.

In 1745 a letter in the Gentleman's Magazine called for Christchurch Harbour to be developed. John Smeaton, the lighthouse builder, reported on Christchurch Harbour in 1762 and in 1771 the canal builder Brindley surveyed the Avon. However, no further major works were carried out. Nevertheless navigation was at one time possible to Salisbury and such navigation was based upon both use and statute. Some few years ago the journey was made by canoe.

There were further plans for a harbour development a century later. Plans by W. Armstrong and B. Tucker were put to a public meeting in November 1836. That year J. Sylvester made a plan for dredging to enable coasters to reach the Town Quay. The following year these plans were modified for the harbour to be used by pleasure craft. In 1845 there was a proposal for a rail link to Mudeford and the construction of a deep water dock there. Some years later there was a proposal for a rail link from Christchurch to Barn Bight at Hengistbury Head and a deep water dock there. Fortunately none of these plans came to fruition. The harbour entrance has since suffered from the erosion caused by Holloway's iron mining and the removal of ironstone from Hengistbury Head in the mid nineteenth century.

The money and numbers of the smugglers could often cause revenue officers to avoid their duty. The Customs Collector at Poole was dismissed in 1678 for collusion with smugglers and the Collector at Weymouth was reported 'seldom sober'. Other Crown servants had their own perks. In 1682 the Captain of Hurst Castle refused to permit the Customs to search there. The same year John Wills was caught ferrying cargo ashore from the *Vine,* ketch, off Studland. He confessed to also transferring cloth from the *Little John* off Hengistbury Head to Poole, on behalf of John Carter a merchant and magistrate. Carter's gang wore masks and carried swords and clubs and were able to terrorise the area. They are known to have hidden goods at the Kings Arms at Poole Quay. During their time the Surveyor at Poole was dismissed for corruption and the Captain of a Poole revenue vessel dismissed for fraud. They were probably not part of the famous Cornish Carter family who had their own warehouse and gun battery at Prussia Cove.

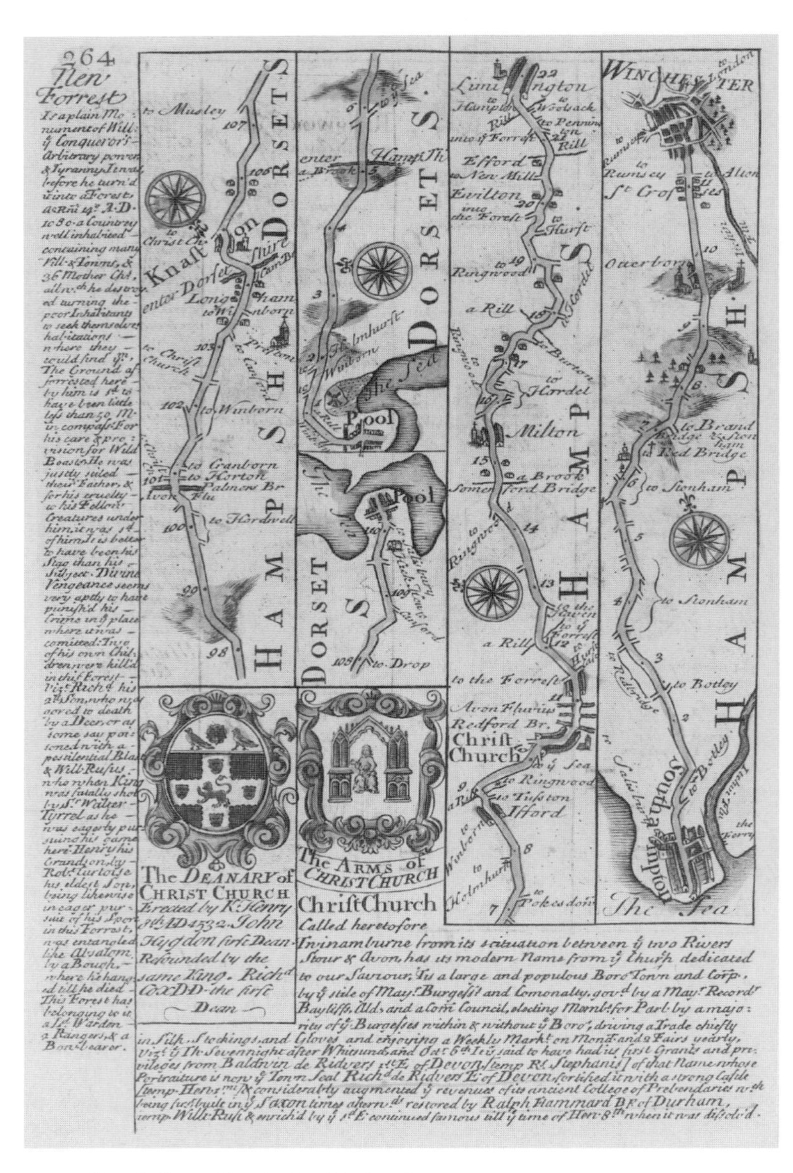

Road Map: Poole to Christchurch to Lymington c. 1700
(Shows seals of Deanary and of Priory of Christchurch)

Two members of a Carter family had been mayors of Christchurch in Tudor times.

Another Poole smuggler was Robert Bennet who used the cellars of the George Inn on Poole Quay. With local magistrates, revenue officials and merchants hand-in-glove with the smugglers, (often in fact they were the smugglers), it is not surprising that in 1698 the Customs Commissioners set up a fleet of sloops to be a Waterguard. In the following year a mounted guard of Riding Officers was in place to patrol the shores. Even so, some coastal towns like Christchurch were in the complete control of the smugglers. In 1691 there is a record of tobacco being shipped to Weymouth from Christchurch.

Poole and Christchurch Bays were well situated for vessels crossing the English Channel. The prominent Hengistbury Head being in the centre opening out from the Isle of Wight, St. Catherine's Point and The Needles to starboard and St. Aldhelm's Head and the Isle of Purbeck to port. Smuggler's landing beaches were potential invasion points guarded by pillboxes and tank traps in the Second World War.

Smugglers did not have it all their own way. In 1699 the customs boat at Hurst made seizures of wine, linen and other French goods from the ship *Norrington* at Keyhaven and from the *Mary Ann* of Lymington.

'Free Trade' goods would be run ashore at convenient points. Swanage, Smugglers Bank at Studland and Wareham Quay in the west required smuggled goods to be taken inland via Wareham and Wool. Landings at Hamworthy would use the Blandford Road whereas Poole Quay had the Wimborne and Ringwood Roads. Landings at Sandbanks, Flag Head Chine, The Ravine, Branksome Chine, Alum Chine, Middle Chine, Durley Chine, Bourne Mouth, Boscombe Chine and Honeycomb Chine were probably controlled from De Coy Pond Cottage. Western Shore (of Christchurch) at White Pits, Southbourne; Double Dykes at Hengistbury Head and Wick all gave access to Iford and Castle Lane. The east landing of Wick Ferry at Christchurch, north of Quomps, Town Quay, Fisherman's Bank at Stanpit, Mudeford Quay, Avon Beach, Friars Cliff, Chewton Bunny, Beckton Bunny, Taddiford Gap (aka Paddy's Gap), Milford-on-Sea and Hurst Spit all used routes to the New Forest. There were staging posts at places such as Sway and Bransgore, often via suitable inns. Such inns included the Cat and Fiddle at Hinton and the Queen's Head at Burley, which were on the route to the unofficial free market at Ridley Wood in the New Forest. Goods would also be taken to Fordingbridge for carriage to Salisbury, and on to Marlborough for Bath and Bristol, or Oxford and the Midlands.

Churches would also be used to store goods en-route. Examples include the churches at: Langton Matravers, Studland, Kinson, Sopley and Boldre. A smuggler named Butler once made a run at Christchurch Quay on a Sunday morning. He carried his goods through the Priory churchyard as the congregation left the church. Various places were used as hides, ranging from church towers and crypts to drains, as with the drains under Poole Quay; wine cellars, ice houses as at Stourfield Woods and especially made dry wells. Sometimes chambers were constructed from genuine wells, as at the eastern side of the site of the Fountain Inn at Christchurch. A similar hide was found near the inn at Iford. The cellars of former breweries could also be used as at Bow House and Square House at Christchurch. Hides could also be made under new property, as was the case with the house of Tregonwell's butler at Bournemouth.

Smugglers could be well connected. One who had served in the Coastguard became a Plymouth shipbroker, his brother in the Royal Navy rose to be an Admiral. Lt. Shore RN, later a Commander and subsequently Lord Teignmouth, who was for eight years an Inspecting Officer of Coastguards, wrote that smuggling was characterised by 'utter lawlessness'. Besides men like Tregonwell, other owners of new large homes near the coast with sea views could be involved in smuggling, as perhaps at Avonmouth (now a respectable hotel) at Mudeford and the Priory House built by Gustav Brander.

Besides the risks of the sea there remained the risks of war. In 1690 a French fleet appeared in Poole Bay and the town stood by on 21st June to resist a landing, which did not take place. In 1694 a French privateer seized a Weymouth fishing ketch; the privateer was attacked by the *Sea Adventurer* of Poole and driven ashore at Lulworth. King William III awarded a gold chain to the victorious captain. The next year a Poole fishing boat with two guns and some small arms was attacked by a French privateer, but turned the tables and the fisher boat captured the privateer.

Both sides employed private ships of war - privateers. They were first recorded in 1243 when Henry III issued 'letters of marque and reprisal'. Between 1626 and 1629 some 14 Poole ships were privateers. English ships could act as privateers for foreign countries not at war with England. Some were virtually licensed pirates. Members of the Court owned privateers and members of the gentry invested in them. Such vessels were difficult to

Mudeford, 1861; from Haven Quay to the mouth of the Mude
(Shows Avonmouth Hotel and mouth of the Bure).

control and like some Royal Navy vessels they engaged in smuggling. However, they were a cheap and convenient way for governments to wage war at sea. As late as 1804 Lord Nelson wrote, 'The conduct of all privateers is ..... so near piracy that I only wonder any civilised nation can allow them'.

The newly formed Waterguard soon had casualties: the customs boat from Shoreham was lost with all hands in 1702. The Great Storm of 26th November 1703 cost the lives of many seamen; some 300 ships sank in the English Channel. In 1704, in an appalling tragedy, 22 revenue men were drowned in the Bristol Channel, and in 1706 the Shoreham boat was again lost with only one survivor. The smugglers also took lives: the mate of the customs yacht *Greenhill* was murdered at Cowes in 1716. In 1720 another officer was murdered, and his widow and orphans had to petition the Customs Commissioners for a pension; at the time £7 and 10 shillings was paid to the widow and 30 shillings a year for each child. There was no certain pension for the dependants of officers killed on service until 1780.

The risk was not just to the Waterguard: in 1717 a Riding Officer (coastal patrol duty) was murdered by smugglers in Sussex. Also in that year another officer lost an eye and still another was kicked in the face. In the following year an officer had his right arm broken in two places and other wounds. It was safer to collude with smugglers than to fight them. In 1719 the Riding Officer at Lulworth was suspected of collusion with local smugglers, hence he was posted to Christchurch!

In 1717 the Collector at Weymouth reported 'The smugglers ride with companies of armed men 20,30 or 40 in a gang and very dangerous to the Officers in the night time'. Later he reported '... they [smugglers] bid defiance to all law and government. They come very often in gangs of 60 to 100 men to the shore in disguise armed with swords, pistols, blunderbusses, carbines and quarterstaffs ... Carry off goods .... in defiance of Officers ... beat, knock down and abuse whoever they meet ... so that travelling by night near the coast, and the peace of the country, are become very precarious ...' One run was of five ships simultaneously, described as 'a perfect fair at the waterside'.

The first of the Hovering Acts was introduced, in 1718, to prevent small vessels running spirits into shallow creeks, or loitering close to land to run goods ashore when the coast was clear of revenue men. No vessel under 15 tons could legally import spirits as cargo, and vessels were liable to seizure. Lawful traders found they could not compete with duty free goods. Traders in Poole made petitions to this end in 1720, 1722 and 1728. Perhaps that is

Poole Harbour Office and Custom House c. 1900

Guinea Boat - Galley, off Dorset Cliffs, c. 1800

By kind permission of Mary Evans Picture Library, Blackheath, London

one reason why Poole had a Custom House built in 1730. It burnt down in 1813, after which the present building was erected (now a wine bar).

The number of oars in an unlicensed galley was limited to six in 1721. All others found within two leagues (six miles) offshore could be seized. This was to prevent multi-oared galleys being built which could outrun a sailing vessel in a calm, or pull into the eye of the wind in a breeze so that a square rigged vessel could not follow, or a fore and aft rig would have to tack. Illegal galleys were built up to 40 feet long with a narrow 7 feet beam. With a crew of 20 or more it made them fast if somewhat unstable. Hengistbury Head is only about 70 miles from Cherbourg; with a good crew able to sprint at nine and a half knots, if chased, the journey could take one night. Unlicensed galleys remained a threat to the revenue until the age of steam power. They were a particular risk in illegal exports of bullion. In the Napoleonic Wars they were known as 'guinea boats', from the sovereigns carried in money belts by the smugglers, (a certain drowning in a capsize).

Daniel Defoe on his travels in 1714 wrote of Lymington, 'any foreign commerce except it be what we call smuggling ... the reigning commerce of this part of the ... coast'.

In 1733 Southampton smugglers beat up customs men using holly clubs and loaded whips, so that two revenue men died of their wounds. The following year the crew of the *Calshot* customs vessel mutinied and were dismissed. In order to give some protection to officers, in 1736 the death sentence was introduced for wounding a revenue man. For resisting a seizure the penalties could be transportation, imprisonment or hard labour.

The Excise seized smuggled tea from the home of a customs man at Abbotsbury in 1737. Sometimes there was no love lost between the two revenue services.

In 1738 the *Beehive* customs sloop called for help from *HMS Diamond* cutter. The *Diamond* sent a boat to board a smuggler. However, in the dark the smugglers captured a naval officer and four men and made their escape. The Royal Navy men were put ashore at Boulogne. It was reported, in 1744, that a large gang of smugglers operated in the Christchurch area protected by ships' guns and small arms.

The Duke of Richmond's Act of 1746 provided that a known smuggler should have his name published in the *London Gazette*; if he did not surrender within 40 days he could be liable to death. A reward of £500 was offered to help catch such men. This draconian measure was little used but the violent nature of smuggling justified its passage.

One of the worst gangs was the Hawkhurst Gang based in the Weald of Kent. In 1744 the gang captured four revenue men at Shoreham, stealing their arms and horses. Two of the revenue men had formerly been smugglers; they were tied to a tree and whipped near to death, then kidnapped to France. The gang had been led by a highwayman called Gray. Besides smuggling they engaged in burglary, armed robbery, torture and murder. They terrorised the village of Goudhurst, but the villagers were organised by an ex-soldier called Sturt, and the gang under a new leader, Thomas Kingsmill, was defeated in a pitched battle in 1746. Two people, including Kingsmill's brother, were killed.

On 22 September 1747 the *Swift,* revenue cutter, chased the *Three Brothers* from Guernsey seeking to make a run near Christchurch. The chase took place from 5 pm to 11 pm and the smuggler was fired upon before she struck. The Dorset smugglers lost a cargo of two tons of tea, 39 casks of brandy and a bag of coffee beans, which were seized and lodged in the Custom House at Poole Quay. The Dorset men turned for help to the Hawkhurst Gang who wished to restore their image after their defeat at Goudhurst.

On 5th October, 30 to 60 smugglers assembled at Rowlands Castle in Hampshire. The mounted gang were heavily armed and had spare arms and ammunition on a pack horse. They rode to Lyndhurst and onto Poole, arriving at about 11pm. The Custom House was shut but an RN sloop was alongside the quay. The gang waited until 2 o'clock in the morning so that the ebb tide lowered the vessel below the quay, thus masking her guns. They then broke into the Custom House, removed 38 cwt. of tea and made off to Fordingbridge where they rested. There, one of the smugglers named Diamond, (aka Dymer, aka The Shepherd), saw an elderly shoemaker acquaintance named Chater and threw him a bag of tea. Chater must have talked since the Customs Collector at Southampton heard the story and sent for Chater to question him. Meantime, Diamond had been arrested on suspicion at Chichester. He eventually turned King's Evidence. In February 1748 Chater was sent towards Chichester for further questioning. He travelled under the escort of a Customs Tide Waiter, called Galley.

Chater and Galley lost their way and were directed to the White Hart at Rowlands Castle where the landlady's two sons were smugglers. These men heard the story and sent for others in the gang. The witness and the revenue man were captured through being made drunk. The smugglers' wives called for the informer and his escort to be hung. The two men were dragged out into a bitter winter night by 14 smugglers to be kicked, whipped and slashed across the face with spurs. They were then both put onto one horse with their legs tied together; they were whipped again and slid down so that their heads were at ground level and struck by the hooves of the horse. They were pulled upright and whipped again so that once more they slipped head first below the horse's belly. They were then each put tied behind a smuggler and whipped once more. Eventually they were slung off the horses and further beaten. Galley was then attacked about the testicles by Jackson; he was castrated and pleaded to be shot dead. However, he was then buried while still alive at Hartingcombe near Rake. His horse was dismembered to leave no trace. Chater was kept chained to a post for three days in freezing weather at Trotton. He was then beaten, his teeth knocked out and slashed across the face cutting through his nose and almost gouging out his eyes. He was made to pray. Finally he was hung slowly over Harris' Well at Lady Holt Park. After 15 minutes or so of choking he was flung down the dry well and large stones cast down upon him, one of which almost severed a leg. After a tree trunk was thrown onto him he expired.

The same gang suspected a labourer named Hawkins, at Yapton near Chichester, of stealing some of their smuggled tea in January 1748. The unfortunate man was taken to an inn at Slindon Common, kicked in the groin and whipped to death. His body was thrown in a pond at Parkam Park.

There was public outrage at these sadistic murders and some of the gang were brought to trial. Seven of them were sentenced to death at Chichester on 18th January 1749. One, Jackson, a main torturer, died before sentence could be carried out. Three others including Kingsmill, were sent to the Old Bailey for trial. They were executed at Tyburn on 26th April that year, their bodies to be hung in chains. They scoffed that they would not rot in the ground. Four others of the gang were hung for highway robbery and two more for housebreaking. Three others escaped from jail.

Despite such use of capital punishment, smuggling continued. The *Westminster Journal* in January 1748 reported ' ... scarce a week passes but great quantities of goods are run between Lymington and Christchurch ....'

That same year a smuggling vessel, the *Charles,* a fishing boat from Guernsey, was chased off Portland. The smugglers ran their craft ashore at Bourne Heath (Bournemouth) and fled on foot. The vessel and its cargo were taken to Poole. The smugglers' profit justified their risk. For example, in 1750 duty paid tea cost seven shillings a pound, whereas duty free tea was two shillings a pound. By 1780 two thirds of all tea was smuggled.

In Lulworth a revenue man was thrown over a cliff, not an unusual fate for customs officers in the criminal heyday from the mid 1600s to the mid 1800s. Other examples include customs officers thrown over the cliffs at High Downs and their bodies lost in the sea and a preventive officer being stoned to death at Totland Bay on the Isle of Wight. For revenue men there was a real risk of being beaten, clubbed, stabbed, shot, drowned, thrown over cliffs or otherwise wounded or murdered. It is little wonder that some felt discretion to be the better part of valour.

In 1758 at Batsman's Chine (Branksome?) between Sandbanks and Bournemouth, the father of the later famous Isaac Gulliver led 24 smugglers to attack three revenue men to rescue a seizure of tea and liquor.

Three customs men had a seizure at Branksome Chine rescued in 1760 by 30 smugglers armed with metal-shod 'bats', the name given to staves or quarter-staffs. They left one tub of brandy as a consolation prize.

Smugglers were always concerned to deter informers. In 1762 William Manuel of Iford, near Christchurch, was suspected as being a likely informer. Eight men broke into his home and his teenage son was kidnapped to ensure his silence. The youth, Joseph Manuel, was taken to the cottage later known as Decoy House, at De Coy Pond, Bourne Heath. From there he was shipped to Alderney and used as a slave. Eventually the boy escaped, from Jersey, but with severe injuries. In 1766 one of the men responsible, named Kirby, was captured at Swanage. In another case smugglers whipped to death a man they suspected of being an informer.

In 1762 smugglers near Poole landed a run from the *Ranger* a Guernsey based privateer. This use of a government registered vessel caused consternation to officialdom. Also in that year a cargo of tea was recovered by smugglers after its seizure at Canford. During a run in 1763, at Watering (Alum?) Chine between Bournemouth and Sandbanks some 40 smugglers made three revenue men hold their horses while they landed three tons of tea. Sometimes tea was adulterated to increase its volume. Such 'smooch' was made in the Wimborne area by the use of mouldy leaves and sheep dung.

Samuel Hookey of Wick is said to be a well-known Christchurch smuggler. A man with this name was mayor in 1718, 1727 and 1743. The story is that he

Brownsea Castle
Engraving of drawing by J.P. Neale, 1810.

Also in 1770 Richard Hughes of Wick, Christchurch, petitioned for a troop of dragoons to be stationed at Christchurch in order to provide some security to local people from smugglers gangs; but at that time with no result. In October that year, dragoons at Blandford refused to turn out to assist customs men against smugglers. In December the following year the Collector at Poole asked for dragoons to be based at Wimborne, owing to the 'great and desperate gangs of smugglers'. The smugglers' private armies 200 strong meant that many coastal areas were in virtual anarchy. Magistrates did not enforce seizures; when the lugger *Lottery* was seized at Hurst her gear was removed to a private house but the Justice would not permit its seizure.

In 1772 at Stokes Bay, Portsmouth, a revenue boat crew of seven men attempted to prevent a run but were stopped by 60 smugglers on horse-back, who rescued about half the seized goods, leaving the revenue men wounded, one with a broken arm. Also in that year a party of customs officers were attacked at Southampton and one officer died of his wounds.

In January 1774 the excise cutter *Anson* brought a seizure of 164 casks of geneva and 2675 lb. tea into Poole. Jack Rattenbury, the famous Devonshire smuggler, made his first ever run, around 1774, which was into Christchurch by open boat. The run was successful but later he was captured and then managed to escape. Smugglers sometimes travelled in disguise or masked. It is reported that a miller of Christchurch, so disguised, overpowered two revenue men on Bourne Heath and left them tied up until they were found the next morning.

Smugglers' prices were low and attracted customers from all classes of society. In 1776 their prices at Weymouth were: cask brandy 16/6d gallon, cask rum 15/6d gallon and Bohea tea 1/4d lb. In that year the Parish Clerk of Christchurch asked the vicar, the Reverend William Jackson, if smuggling was a sin. When the clergyman replied that it was, the Clerk protested, 'Lord have mercy on the town of Christchurch. Who is there who has not had a tub [of spirits].'

In 1777 a wagon with 60 casks was seized by four Christchurch officers at White Pitts on the Western Shore (Southbourne) near Christchurch. However, 19 smugglers then rescued the seizure and beat up the officers. A Riding Officer, named Bursey, was amongst those attacked, wounded and disarmed. However, he gave chase and shot a smuggler's horse. Other casks, 25 in total, were seized having been left on the beach. This brave officer was later murdered in cold blood. In June that year a Dunkirk schooner landed 20 tons of tea at Arish Mells in sight of the customs who decided not to interfere because the vessel aimed her 24 pounders on the beach. The smugglers removed three wagons of tea but left 12 cwt. on the beach which was seized. This seizure was then rescued by 30 or 40 of the smugglers who beat and cut the officers. The following year smugglers from Verwood recovered seizures by breaking and entering the house of the Excise Supervisor at Blandford.

Poole privateers were active. The lugger *Lottery* at Poole was renamed *Tyger* and operated as a private ship of war. In August 1778 the *Tyger* brought in the French vessel *Prosperity* with 87 tons of brandy and the following month a Dutch vessel in French trade laden with salt. In October the *Defiance* brought in a brig laden with ship building materials.

In November 1778 the *Salisbury and Winchester Journal* reported as follows: 'Last Sunday the largest seizure was made between Lymington and Christchurch that has been known for many years by the Custom House officers and two companies of the Lancashire Militia. It is said that there were three cargoes, two of which the smugglers got off and had just landed the third and loaded twelve wagons besides a vast number of horses. One of the smugglers fired a blunderbuss at the soldiers first and wounded one of them in the arm, the soldiers immediately returned the fire and killed Farmer Barnes, a smuggler, who was shot through the heart and the head at the same moment. The twelve loaded wagons were brought to this port (Southampton) together with 50 horses and it is said there is a great quantity of lace, besides tea and spirits'. The last weekly paper of the month gave further details: 'Last week the Lancashire Militia (which were quartered at Romsey, Lymington and Christchurch since the camp broke up at Winchester) began their march in three divisions for their own county. A correspondent has favoured us with a particular and authentic account of the late seizure of smuggled goods at Lymington, being the greatest ever made in that part of the kingdom, viz. 4 wagons and 4 carts drawn by 33 horses, in which were 46 small casks containing 172 gallons brandy; 34 casks - 123 gallons rum, 43 casks - 161 gallons geneva, 510 oil-case bags - 13,232 lb. tea, 61 ditto with 1,584 lb. green tea; 6 ditto - 282 lb. raw coffee. All which goods were safely lodged in the King's Custom House at Southampton the following day and will be sold by public auction in a few weeks'. The casks in the report are clearly 4 gallon tubs.

In 1778 two Spanish brigs were wrecked in Christchurch Bay and France joined America in war against Britain. Smugglers could then apply for Letters of Marque as privateers and so arm themselves officially. The next year the privateer *Oxford* bought into Poole the French vessel *Gibroeders*. However it was not one-sided; many Poole vessels were taken by French privateers. The British Royal Navy successfully blockaded the French Republican Navy but French privateers from small harbours made many captures among British cargo vessels. Also in 1779 the Spanish joined the war against Britain and by 1780 there were estimated to be 30 armed smuggling vessels operating off the coast of Dorset.

From 1779 a uniform was introduced for customs officers on revenue vessels as an aid to recognition of their authority. In that year at Blackwater, near Hurn at Christchurch, eight officers and two soldiers of the South Lincoln Militia seized 77 bags of tea but the smugglers rescued 33 bags. The same year 40 or 50 smugglers attacked an excise officer and six dragoons at Cranborne Chase. Numbers told, and despite having one killed and one badly wounded, the smugglers rescued their goods and made off with the dragoons' horses, which were recovered the next day. Still in 1779 the revenue and dragoons fought smugglers at Wool, killing one and wounding several; 32 horses, 2,300 lb. of tea and 300 gallons of brandy and gin were seized. Because of the war with France two of the revenue vessels at Poole, the *Antelope* and the *Roebuck*, were taken into the Royal Navy.

Also in 1779 the *Phoenix,* lugger, 96 tons, pierced for oars, was seized in Christchurch Harbour for carrying casks of brandy, rum and gin concealed in a cargo of grain. The vessel was released on payment of a £55 penalty. It was seized again in 1783. This vessel was again taken in 1784 at the Battle of Mudeford (see later). It appears that the owner, Streeter, must have purchased the *Phoenix* back at auctions of seized vessels in 1779 and 1783. The problem with guinea boat galleys had become so great in the short sea crossing that galleys were limited to four oars off the coast of Kent, but six oars were still permitted off Hampshire.

Smugglers captured during the war ran a strong risk of being pressed i.e. forced to join the Royal Navy. There is no doubt about the consequences for the families of pressed men. Their loved ones and financial help dis-appeared, perhaps for years, perhaps forever. Pressed men could not expect leave, and were subject to the full rigours of harsh naval discipline backed by the lash and the noose. Smugglers' families in such a case had to rely on their own efforts and the help of relatives and friends, if they had any, or seek parish relief. In one awful case the 19-year-old wife of a pressed man with two infant children and debts found herself destitute, starving in rags. She was caught shop-lifting and sentenced to death. She was taken to the place of execution with a baby at her breast.

Dragoons assisting The Revenue to make a seizure
By kind permission of the Board of Trustees of the National Museums and Galleries.
(H.M. Customs and Excise National Museum)

The Press Gang were liable to descend on any small or large town and seize all seamen who did not carry a protection letter from a Port Admiral. The Press Gang were based at Poole and at Lymington. At the latter they were based at the Old Harlequin Inn, Lymington Quay. RN vessels at sea also pressed men from cargo vessels nearing their voyage end. In May 1790 a Jersey vessel had all her crew taken from her off The Needles, apart from her master and cabin boy. The passengers, who included the Governor of Jersey, had to work the ship to Southampton. The RN vessel *Seagull* captured a smuggling cutter *Diana* and pressed all her men. In 1779 four pressed men were being taken through the New Forest from Lymington to Southampton when they were rescued by armed horsemen, probably smugglers from their gang.

In January 1780 Paul Jones, the American, was in action with his squadron against British shipping off the Isle of Wight. Two months later the Collector at Poole reported ' ... smugglers ... so notoriously daring, abusive and insolent that it is extremely hazardous for any number of revenue officers, without the assistance of the military, to attempt to attack them, or even to be seen at or near some of the places they reside'. The Poole cutter *Unicorn* bought in an American schooner as a prize, in May. The *Union* cutter also brought an American prize into Poole in the same month. In June two French frigates chased and fired upon a Poole privateer and in the following month a French lug sail privateer was operating in Poole and Christchurch Bays.

In 1780 officers seized 1871 lb. of coffee and 541 gallons of brandy and rum at Kinson. During the same year smugglers again broke into warehouses at Poole and rescued the seizures. On 24th August, John Bursey, the brave Riding Officer, was murdered at Chewton. (This was in the parish of Milton until the formation of Highcliffe Parish in 1845). He was called from his home by two men who said they wished to claim a reward for finding smuggled goods in a nearby barn. Bursey was then beaten about the head in front of his wife and children, receiving seven fractures of the skull, he died three days later despite the expenditure of 11 guineas on a nurse and a doctor from Christchurch. His distraught wife, Lydia, sought to intervene but had a blunderbuss fired at her when she cried out 'murder' from a window. The murderers then threatened to kill her and her five children. In 1782 an attempt to bring the murderers to justice failed through lack of evidence and the case against the two men, Bungey and Wilkins, was dropped.

It was not until December 1780 that the Customs Commissioners decided to pay a disability pension to men injured on service. They agreed to award £10 per annum to those who lost a hand or foot or greater injury, and to pay surgeons' bills for other wounds. A mariner on the *Laurel* of Poole lost his left eye in action in 1783 and so may have benefited. Such awards were not automatic. (When the author was serving as an Officer of Customs and Excise at Cowes he found a letter book containing the copy of a request by the late eighteenth century Collector, William Arnold, for a pension for a customs boatman who had lost both hands when seeking to climb the side of a smuggler's lugger. The letter book was sent to the museum at Kings Beam House, the Customs and Excise H.Q. in London. The office at Cowes also contained a metal Tudor chest for use as a Queen's Warehouse to store small high value seizures. The chest was made in metal bands to imitate wood and had two enormous locks. The idea was to use it as a safe, and fill it with cannon balls so it would be too heavy to steal). In Arnold's day the pension for a widow had increased to £15 a year and fifty shillings was paid for each orphan aged under 15. Until 1820 widows' pensions ceased on re-marriage.

One evening in 1780 the elderly Edward Hooper, owner of Hurn Court near Christchurch, a magistrate and a Commissioner of Customs, was giving dinner to his kinsman Lord Shaftesbury, when a smugglers' convoy passed the grounds of the house. Hooper resolutely refused to look out of the window, so that when an officer of dragoons called later to ask if smugglers had passed, the Commissioner was able to say he had seen nothing. Such dereliction of duty at such a high level can only have been increased at lower levels in society, the law and the customs service.

The revenue vessel *Swift* was ordered to patrol between Lymington and Portland to prevent the illegal export of wool. However in March 1781 she was taken by a French privateer. Also in March the Poole Customs were assisted by the Nottinghamshire Militia in making a seizure. The troops then got drunk on the seized brandy. On 17th March the passage vessel from Poole to Portsmouth was taken off Christchurch Head by a French vessel. The prize was abandoned when a lugger came up but all except one of her crew were carried to France. In April the revenue cutters *Laurel*, *Rose* and *Speedwell* were in action off the Isle of Wight. The following year the Camarthanshire Militia were stationed at Poole.

Local revenue cutters were: *Swan* based at Cowes; *Rose* (16 guns, 190 tons) from Southampton; *Speedwell* (16 guns, 194 tons, 31 crew), and *Diligence* both at Weymouth; *Laurel* (131 tons) and *Garland* both based at Poole. In 1784 the *Alarm* and the *Spider* were also at Poole.

Smugglers Intrusion
Engraving of a painting by Sir David Wilkie RA, c.1820
By kind permission of the British Museum, London.

Much larger vessels were needed to be adequately armed and crewed if they were to be able to fight vessels of 200 or 300 tons, with crews of 100 men armed with as many as 24 guns, each of up to 12 pounds or more weight of shot. Such large vessels would on occasion convoy smaller smuggling craft to protect them from revenue cruisers and French privateers. For example, the customs cutter *Rose* took a new 200 ton smuggling lugger of 14 guns (10 mounted) in Studland Bay, in July 1781, killing two and wounding six of her crew and capturing a cargo of tea, spirits and bale goods. Some of the smuggling crew were ashore and so escaped. However, in January the following year, the *Rose* was in action with a smuggling vessel off The Needles which mounted 24 carriage guns besides swivels. After one and a half hours of action the *Rose* had to sheer off with several of her men dead and wounded.

In June 1781 a Dunkirk privateer armed with 18 x 9 pdr. guns was taken by a ruse used by two more weakly-armed customs cutters. One cutter had pretended to be a smuggler and fled before the other who hoisted her chase pennant and fired her guns but without shot. The Dunkirker sought to aid what appeared to be a smuggler and was then attacked by both cutters.

The types of craft used varied according to availability. Both revenue and smugglers built clinker hull, single mast, deep keel, fast cutters with a long bowsprit, capable of 12 knots. Only the revenue were permitted to have sprits of more than two-thirds the length of the hull. No jib was permitted on the bowsprit, hence no flying jib sail. However, a jib topsail was legal. The smugglers also favoured fast shallow draft, three short-mast luggers with bow and gaff sprits. Such vessels could take the shore easily and unload directly onto a beach. For example, Slippery Rogers of Christchurch had a 120 foot lugger, measured from the tip of the bowsprit to the end of the gaff outrigger boom, an open-hull vessel apart from a cuddy fore and aft to give some protection from weather. The absence of a deck amidships enabled the bulk storage and swift unloading of cargo, up to 3,000 ankers (8½ gallon casks). The lugger could be rowed by 40 oarsmen. It was often moored at Christchurch Quay, but was eventually wrecked attempting to land cargo in bad weather. Perhaps it went to grief on the Christchurch Ledge. Fast doubled ended yawls with two lugsail masts were also used. Such 70 foot open boats could easily carry 1,000 casks of spirits and run right ashore before unloading. Luggers and yawls were designed on the lines of old Norse vessels, seaworthy yet capable of being grounded on the shore.

Slippery Rogers, the lugger owner, may have sprung from the Rogers family who gave Christchurch mayors eleven times in the seventeenth century.

REVENUE CRUISER CHASING SMUGGLING LUGGER.

Before firing on a smuggler the cruiser was bound to hoist his Revenue colours —both pennant and ensign—no matter whether day or night.

(From the original painting by Charles Dixon, R.I.)

Revenue cutter in chase of a smugglers lugger

By kind permission of the Board of Trustees of the National Museums and Galleries (H.M. Customs and Excise National Museum).

Perhaps he had an ancestor in Henry Rogers of Hoburne whose tomb has been mentioned.

Besides sailing craft the smugglers also used long, narrow, shallow draught, very fast galleys of 12 or more oars, with a removable lug sail mast. These were often unlicensed and such galleys over 28 feet long were illegal. Low-lying vessels like these were hard to see, especially at night. They could lose a sail boat by pulling into the eye of the wind. With doubled oarsmen they could do nine and a half knots. Such 'guinea-boats' were possibly made at Gervis Point (near where the Black House now stands), on Mudeford Spit at Christchurch Harbour. Gigs as little as 14 feet long were also used to cross the Channel or to meet ships at sea, and smuggle back 20 tubs of spirits. Such craft operated out of Bembridge on the Isle of Wight. Vessels were built at Gervis Point for many years. Records show that a 200 ton vessel *The Lady Canning* which was wrecked 1861 was built there in 1842, and in 1848 the 96 foot long brig *Enterprise* (condemned 1864) was built. Both were far too big for use in Christchurch Harbour.

Smugglers were reported by Napoleon to have done great mischief to the British Government. He said, 'they [English] have the courage and ability to do anything for money'. Smugglers carried in spies and carried out escaped French prisoners of war. They transported a wide variety of goods which, since duty free, were a form of economic warfare. Some 40 million francs worth of goods were exported from France by smugglers annually during the wars between the years: 1778-83, 1793-1802, 1803-14 and in 1815. They carried intelligence to the enemy by letters and through newspapers, but perhaps most important of all they carried out gold bullion. A British sovereign sold for thirty shillings in France, a 50% increase. Gold coins to the value of £10,000 or more were sold each week. Bullion smugglers could be paid by an order on a bank or in kind by brandy or lace. Much of the money Napoleon used to finance his return from Elba was raised in London. At one time Napoleon had a camp for 500 British smugglers at Dunkirk and later at Gravelines.

The smugglers' rate of profit could be about 500% and he could afford to risk losing one cargo in six. He still made a profit if he lost one cargo in three. The method was that the Venturer raised the finance; contributions and payments were made by the Bagman and the Captain bought the cargo 'in foreign' and ran it to the shore in his ship. The Spotter on shore called in the ship by light when the coast was clear. The Lander took the goods from the ship on the beach and arranged transportation - men, horses, wagons and hiding places. The Batman was the enforcer, such men carried 6 feet long quarter-staffs topped with iron; the Wagoners (two to each) carried loaded whips and other weapons; the smuggling crews had side arms as well as their ship's guns.

The main foreign entrepôts used were: Roscoff, St. Malo, Channel Isles, Cherbourg, Barfleur, Le Havre, Dieppe, Boulogne, Calais, Gravelines, Dunkirk, Newport, Ostende, Flushing and Antwerp. Smuggled brandy was known as 'Nantz' from the French town of Nantes; cognac was nicknamed Cousin Jack. A four gallon tub of spirits sold at sea, for example to a fisherman, cost 10/6d, having cost the smuggler 7/6d at Cherbourg. If landed between Hurst and Christchurch the tub would cost a Landsman 14/-. If sold in the Isle of Wight or Langstone or Portsmouth where control was tighter the price was 21/-.

The development of Roscoff was a direct result of the British Government seeking to install an effective Customs presence in Guernsey. This they attempted in 1709, 1719, 1722 and 1769. Only then was a Registrar's Office for shipping able to be set up. The Channel Islands are of course still not a part of the United Kingdom.

The Government offered The Act of Oblivion in 1782 which gave amnesty for smuggling crimes of up to a £500 fine if one seaman and one landsman were found for the Fleet. Offences above £500 fines would be excused on finding two seamen and two landsmen for the Royal Navy. In the same year Captain Lisle of the customs service reported: ' The smuggling trade between the Isle of Wight and St. Aldhelm's Point is now carried on in large armed cutters and luggers ... with a French Commission ...' He went on to contrast the efficiency of the customs vessels at Poole and Southampton: 'Two revenue cutters ... that from Southampton makes some good seizures the other from Poole very few ... owing to master, mates and crew being corrupted ...'

In 1782 an excise officer had his horse shot from under him; and between Ringwood and Salisbury five revenue men and some soldiers were attacked by 180 smugglers who rescued seizures and wounded two of the officers. In January 1783 Mr Critchell, the Riding Officer at Ringwood, was dragged off his horse and badly beaten, within danger of his life, in the street at Burley in broad daylight. In that year smugglers in Devon captured the boats crew from *Spider*, a revenue cutter, together with a Riding Officer and held them for 36 hours. They beat off an attack by two revenue vessels and ran four tons of tea and 1500 tubs of brandy. The revenue men were cast adrift in a boat with no oars. A similar thing happened off the coast of Essex when

The Batman
By kind permission of the Board of Trustees of the National Museums and Galleries (H.M. Customs and Excise National Museum).

The Tubman

By kind permission of the Board of Trustees of the National Museums and Galleries (H.M. Customs and Excise National Museum).

smugglers captured *Swift*, a revenue cutter, using three smuggling vessels and a French privateer. The crew of *Swift* were cast adrift and the cutter retained for use in smuggling. She was recaptured the following year off Sussex.

By 1783 smugglers in the Christchurch area were using 30 to 40 wagons at a time to smuggle cargoes in daylight. Isaac Gulliver's White Wig Gang ran a cargo at Bourne Bottom (Bournemouth) which required a convoy two miles long to move it all. Gulliver was a very successful smuggler, he avoided personal involvement in violence, leaving that to his underlings. They were a gang of about 40 to 50 men wearing smocks and powdered hair, hence their name - the White Wigs. Gulliver originated from Semington in Wiltshire; married the daughter of a publican at Thorney Down and moved to West Moors and Corfe Mullen. Later he owned property at Long Critchel, Longham and Kinson. At one time he hid from the revenue by posing as a shepherd in Wimborne market. On another occasion he is said to have lain in a coffin and posed as dead. He took a pardon under the Act of Oblivion by providing substitutes for the Royal Navy. He died in his bed at the age of 77 in 1822 and is buried at Wimborne Minster. There are many stories about Gulliver. One tale says that he was an illegitimate child sired by one of the Matravers family; another story is that he revealed a French plot to kidnap or murder George III from his yacht off Weymouth and so was permitted to continue his smuggling career.

In October 1783 Collector Arnold at Cowes reported ' ... smuggling has increased on this coast to an alarming degree. Illicit trade is principally carried on in large armed cutters or luggers from 200 to 300 tons burthen with which the revenue cutters are not able to contend.... It is no unusual thing for them to land their goods in open day under the protection of their guns, sometimes in sight of the Revenue vessels, who they will not suffer to come near or board them. The large vessels frequently convey over other smaller vessels. They keep off until the night, when they run in and land their cargoes at places where gangs of smugglers to the number of 200-300 meet them. To such a regular science is smuggling now reduced that we are informed the smugglers have stated prices for their goods in proportion to the distances they bring them. If they sell at sea, the price of a four gallon cask is about half a guinea; if landed on shore 14 shillings to 15 shillings a cask and if brought into town one guinea.' (21/- = £ 1.05) For example, the *Roebuck* revenue cutter came upon a smugglers' cutter armed and with 50 men in Chichester Harbour and was unable to interfere.

High Cliff from the West c. 1790
(Shows the original building, overlooking Christchurch Bay towards Hurst)

Arnold, who was the Collector at Cowes from 1777 to 1800, acted as a contractor and built vessels to engage smugglers. Important builders were Richard Pinney at Poole, later the firm of Pinney and Adams; Thomas Inman at Lymington; John Gely at Cowes; and Thomas White at Cowes, later J. Samuel White and Company.

In his report Collector Arnold referred to the *Cornish Ranger*, a lugger of about 300 tons mounting 36 guns as: 'frequently lands goods between The Needles and Christchurch Head' (i.e. Christchurch Bay). This vessel landed 3,000 casks and 10 or 12 tons of tea in September 1783 during one run and convoyed three smaller luggers. The *Wasp,* 270 tons and 22 guns worked the same area of coast. Arnold complained of a new fine cutter being built at Cowes for the smugglers, the *Favourite* (220 tons and 20 guns). He reported that 70 foot long open boats, apparently legal since pierced for six oars could, by moving the thwarts, pull 12 oars. He recommended stationing an RN frigate and cutter at Studland and an RN cutter in Hurst Roads, to aid the revenue cutters. The stationing of such vessels would delay landings by the smugglers. If landings were delayed for three or four days the smugglers would be frustrated, since they would not be able to keep the landing gangs together on shore for that length of time.

In November 1783, Arnold offered seized cutters for sale at Cowes: the *John and Susannah* (280 tons 22 x 6 pdr.) and the *Achilles* (180 tons, 18 guns 4 and 6 pdr.). Smugglers would often buy back such vessels at auctions of seized goods.

Peace with France in 1783 permitted Royal Navy vessels to be seconded to aid the customs service. *HMS Orestes*, Captain Ellis RN, was one such vessel, based at Cowes. She was a 300 ton, (18 x 9 pdr.) brig-rigged sloop. (RN vessels of less than 29 guns were classed as sloops.) She was painted yellow and pierced for sweeps so that she could work in a calm. Originally she had been the *Mars*, a prize taken from the Dutch. Her complement was six officers, 16 marines and 72 seamen. The *Orestes* was bloodied in May 1784 when smugglers ran down one of her boats. She took a large armed cutter laden with tea, brandy and other duty free goods into Cowes. In June, when off Lulworth, she sent a boat in chase of a smugglers' cutter. The latter fired on the ship's boat without warning, wounding three men, two of them mortally.

Also based at Cowes was the *Swan*, a revenue cutter, operated by the Collector Mr Arnold. The first *Swan* had been wrecked off The Needles on her first patrol, but was replaced by another of the same name. The captain of this *Swan II* customs cutter (90 tons, 10 x 6 pdr., 25 crew), Mr Sarmon, was the brother of the captain of the excise cutter *Resolution* (8 x 4 pdr.) based at Portsmouth. In late May 1784 the *Swan* had one of her boats captured by smugglers. The boat had come upon a tub-boat off Christchurch Head. The smugglers fired and wounded four of the *Swan's* men, all of whom were captured when a second vessel came up. The captives were then sent on board a large armed cutter laying some distance off shore.

In June 1784 *HMS Rambler*, cutter, took a Littlehampton lugger off the Isle of Wight after a three hour chase. The *Rambler* sent a boat to board the lugger and the smugglers resisted. Two of them were killed and their captain desperately wounded before they surrendered. The seizure included 300 tubs of geneva (gin) and 75 bags of tea. In the same month two smugglers were drowned when their boat was towed under water by the speed of a smuggling cutter in Swanage Bay.

The Collector at Poole had the cutter *Laurel*, the Collector at Southampton had the *Rose*. These vessels also had some success in May 1784. A boat from the *Laurel* seized a lugger which was taken into Poole. However, the smugglers rescued their cargo of tea and spirits on the shore at the cost of one dead and several wounded. The *Rose* brought into Southampton a large smuggling brig, with 1,000 kegs of spirit and a quantity of tea, wines, etc. Also based at Cowes at this time was the *Speedwell*.

The Customs Collectors also controlled Supervisors and Riding Officers. The Supervisor at Christchurch was Joshua S. Jeans who had followed his father into the service. Both father and son had been mayors of the Borough of Christchurch, father Thomas six times and Joshua had been mayor four times. Local customs officials were often mayors, as with Abraham Pike in the nineteenth century and James Beattie and the author in the twentieth. Jeans was the Supervisor of the local Riding Officers, from Hurst to the county boundary with Dorset (Christchurch was in Hampshire until 1974). His officers were Newman, Noyce, Reeks and Bursey, the latter probably a relative of the man murdered at Chewton. The Supervisor's office was in Bridge Street, possibly at No. 10 on the north side, although the present building is a replacement after a fire in 1863 burnt out the original thatched building. The Supervisor in 1803, Mr Pike, lived in a cottage on the southeast side of Castle Street.

These officers were supported by a Customs Waiter responsible for the survey of coastwise trading using the harbour and quays at Christchurch. They also used a Searcher at Bourne Bottom. The Customs Collectors controlled Tide Surveyors who examined vessels anchored offshore. Such men had a boat with a Sitter (coxswain) and six boatmen. There were also Tidesmen to keep watch on board while vessels were unloaded. The Collectors also controlled Land Surveyors who examined vessels alongside quays. These Surveyors had Coast Waiters to examine coastwise shipping and Land Waiters to examine vessels from foreign, who in turn had a Searcher (for exports) and a Weigher (for imports) and could also call upon Tidesmen to act as Watchers. A Sitter (cox'n) and customs boat with six oarsmen were each stationed at Lymington, Christchurch and Poole.

It is likely that many in the customs service had been suborned by bribes and intimidated by threats. In some places, as at Christchurch, a 'live and let live' attitude had developed with local revenue men and smugglers. The latter provided the revenue with a percentage of a run, as seizures, to keep the customs men satisfied and so that they could show their masters some results. Also, the revenue men were rewarded by a share in the value of seizures.

Farmers in the Christchurch area assisted smugglers in a variety of ways: by providing muffled harnesses for wagons and horses (using rope instead of leather, putting felt over horseshoes and using well-greased wagons also stifled their noise); by blocking bridges with wagons or flocks of sheep, and concealing horse and cart tracks by driving cattle over muddy roads and onto beaches, and concealing tubs in manure heaps and haystacks. On occasions the stacks of tubs were thatched to appear like the genuine article.

The ability to block bridges was important. Cargoes intended for the New Forest and landed west of Christchurch would face river crossings whichever route they took. The Stour could be crossed at Wick (ferry), Iford Bridge, Blackwater (ferry), Redcliffe (ferry or Riddles Ford) and Longham Bridge. Hurn Bridge or Palmers Ford would be used to cross the Moors River; and the Avon Causeway, Town and Waterloo Bridges, used for the River Avon. Fording places may also have been used on the Avon at Bisterne (Wattons Ford) and Tyrell's Ford.

During the day smuggling vessels at sea could be signalled by firing gorse, or by smoke pots on the old beacon system. At night a lugger offshore would flash a blue light. If the coast was clear a Spotter with a spout lantern to direct the light would signal to call the lugger in 'on the spot'. If the landing place was compromised the smuggler would strike sparks from flints at different locations as a warning to 'flash off' the lugger. Places with cover near the beach, such as at the Double Dykes, were used to conceal horses and men.

Dragoons crossing Town Bridge, Christchurch, c. 1800

It is said that in Christchurch a milkmaid with two buckets of milk on a yoke would go around the town with a number of small wooden balls floating in each bucket. Those who needed to know, knew that the number of balls gave the time of the run when they had to gather tubmen and batmen.

Some smugglers achieved widespread reputations, like the Carter family of Prussia Cove in Cornwall. They had their own coastal battery and warehouse. It is known that they raided the Penzance Custom House. Another, Thomas Johnstone of Lymington, experimented with submarines in France and America. Jack Rattenbury of Devon who also operated out of Lyme Regis, Sturgess of Hamble, Russell from Southampton and Isaac Gulliver of Kinson were all well-known smugglers.

Other notable local smugglers, besides Gulliver, were: Slippery Rogers, John Early, Samuel Hookey, Bone Tucker and John Streeter. The latter owned a tobacco factory which made snuff, close to what is now the Ship and Distress Inn at Stanpit. Streeter worked a well-known ruse of buying some duty paid hogsheads of tobacco, sometimes from the sale of seizures, so that he held some duty paid invoices to give cover to what were, in fact, smuggled goods. So long as his stock did not exceed his duty paid invoices he was safe with material like tobacco which was difficult to identify. Therefore, he needed to hide goods in excess of his duty paid invoice cover by concealing the volume of his business. Streeter's brother-in-law, named Button, was the owner of a smuggling lugger. Streeter was also in league with the Captain of Hurst Castle in smuggling.

Many local inns were involved in the trade, such as the Haven Inn at Mudeford Quay. This was owned by the widow Hannah Sellers, née Houchings, daughter of the landlord of the Lamb Inn at Hoffleet, Winkton. Her sister was married to an excise officer at Wareham. The sea channel to Stanpit (Ship in Distress Inn) is called Mother Sillers Channel from her name (misspelt). The Haven Inn at Mudeford Quay was at this time at the south-east end of the Dutch Houses, on a promontory bounded by The Run, Christchurch Harbour and the Bure Stream (Hob's Bourne). At high tide the Quay and Inn could be cut off from the mainland at Sandhills.

As a successful smuggler Streeter owned two luggers: the 70 foot long, 73 ton, *Civil Usage* (pierced for 20 x 6 pdr. guns, Captain May) and the 90 foot long, 96 ton *Phoenix* (pierced for 22 x 6 pdr. guns, Captain Parrott). A major run was planned for mid July 1784 and Streeter, acting as Lander, had to plan for several hundred men and horses to be on call.

Haven House (Dutch Cottages), Mudeford Quay
Engraving from a painting by J.M. Gilbert, c.1830.

Logistics may help in attempting to compute the size of the cargoes and numbers of men and required to remove it. The tonnage of a vessel could be computed in various ways; one method was to multiply length by breadth by half breadth and then divide by 94, to give tonnage, which was supposed to be 100 cubic feet per ton. A bag of tea weighed 27 lb. and one man could carry five bags. One rule of thumb is to suggest that one ton of cargo required one foot of hull length for a sea-going vessel. The *Civil Usage*, for example, could safely carry 70 tons and the *Phoenix* 90 tons. Such 160 tons of cargo would need 53 three-ton wagons and 106 horses. Pack horses, if they are used, can carry 3 cwt. each whereas a man could carry 1 cwt. (in two 4¼ gallon tubs). Therefore 50 wagons with 100 horses could lift 150 tons. Two hundred pack horses can lift 30 tons and if each horse is led by one man they would lift another 10 tons. With the wagons there would be a total lift of 190 tons. Trained pack horses could be tied in a string of up to a dozen, with one man to lead and another to bring up the rear. Such a system was useful in narrow lanes and bridle paths. The luggers had no deck, this enabled large cargoes to be rapidly unloaded and a crossing in fine summer weather would encourage overloading. Some of the horses would be required for riding to mount the Batmen as advance and rear guards and for the Lander and his mates to keep control over a long convoy. A reasonable estimate of a convoy, therefore, may be 40 two-horse wagons (120 tons), 200 pack horses (30 tons) and 20 riding horses, with two men per wagon, one man (1 cwt.) per pack horse and one man per riding horse. So a total lift of 160 tons with 300 men could be made. Some men and pack horses could make more than one local journey while others would make one longer trip. One account reports the two luggers as being 73 and 96 tons burden, a total of 169 tons. This would require 43 wagons, 306 men and 306 horses using the basis described above. The lugger crews would also assist in landing, so contemporary accounts of 40 to 50 wagons and 300 to 400 men could be generally accurate.

In July 1784 such substantial preparatory arrangements came to the notice of a local Riding Officer, Mr Noyce, who warned his Supervisor at Christchurch, J. S. Jeans. However, the latter was in league with the smugglers and ignored Noyce. Noyce went secretly to Lymington and warned the customs and military there of his concern about a major run being planned. It appears that Christchurch Barracks were not yet occupied by regular troops.

Meantime, each lugger had loaded its cargo at Cherbourg. The total to be run was probably 8 tons of tea and 42,000 gallons of spirit (9,858 tubs = 4,929 cwt. = 246½ tons), hence the vessels had to carry 254½ tons of cargo which shows the rule of thumb method described above was in fact too little. The contemporary accounts of numbers of men, horses and wagons could still be accurate if local journeys were made to remove some of the cargo to local hides before returning for longer trips. This would account for the smugglers being on shore removing cargo for perhaps 36 hours. The extra load carried by the smuggling luggers could also be accounted for by the fact that they only made short trips, unlike distant voyaging vessels, for which the one ton of cargo per one foot of hull may have been valid due to the need for crew quarters and stores. Also in the account of the action that follows it seems that although two luggers were pierced for guns, they did not carry carriage guns or ballast and so lightened could carry extra cargo.

The voyage to Christchurch Harbour took 24 hours and as the luggers unloaded near the harbour entrance they were observed by the excise cutter *Resolution* in the afternoon of 14th July. Since the latter only had a crew of 18 men she could not prevent the run. She sent in a boat but this was warned off by the smugglers so that *Resolution* sailed to seek assistance. She sent a boat to search for the *Orestes* and herself sought out the *Swan*. The three Crown vessels were met together off Christchurch Ledge by 3pm on 16th July.

However, the smugglers had unloaded their cargoes and stacked them near the Haven at Mudeford on 15th July ready for removal. A Riding Officer, named Bursey, was party to Jeans' arrangements with the smugglers and came down to the beach to ensure their percentage of the crop was put to one side for them to seize. These tubs of spirit they would subsequently report as seizures and some would be taken to Poole Custom House to demonstrate that they were apparently doing their jobs properly. Also they would be rewarded by receiving half the value of those seizures they handed in.

The smugglers observed the arrival of *HMS Orestes* and the two revenue cutters and cleared away the last of the run and took in ballast (50 tons of gravel), without which they could not sail (more evidence that they had overloaded). They then realised that they could not escape and warped their empty vessels into the harbour and began to remove all the gear from the luggers: sails, sheets, masts, yards, anchors and so forth. They also sank their ships' boats in the harbour, hoping to recover them later or make their removal more difficult. In order to lessen their losses and get all their cargo away they needed time. To gain this they were prepared to fight.

High Cliff from the East, 1784
(Shows the first building at High Cliff, looking towards Christchurch Harbour)

The naval forces mounted a cutting out expedition. The *Orestes*, *Swan* and *Resolution* sent in their ships' boats, six in all, to row up The Run and enter the Harbour. The smugglers fired upon them from the luggers, sand dunes, a breastwork they threw up on the quay and from the Haven Inn. The marines replied from the boats but the smugglers were under cover. Mr Allen, the 27-year-old Sailing Master of the *Orestes*, was wounded when he leapt out of his boat to prevent it from grounding. When regaining the boat he was wounded, again, fatally. One of the marines was shot in the arm and other sailors were wounded. The surviving midshipman sought to continue the attack, but the Sergeant of Marines with greater experience persuaded him to call it off and get the wounded back to *Orestes* where they could be treated by a surgeon.

During the action Captain William May of *Civil Usage* rode back to Christchurch for more powder as the smugglers were running low at the time. Firing continued for over three hours between 5pm and 9pm. During this time the smugglers also went on removing their gear from the two luggers. When the ships' boats returned, *Orestes* and the cutters fired their main armaments at the smugglers in the dunes and over the heads of those on the luggers (so avoiding damage to what would become prizes). There is no truth in the fable that the two miles distant Priory was struck by cannon shot. The smugglers then withdrew and the ships' boats returned to take possession and tow the prizes out of the harbour.

It has been alleged that *HMS Orestes* fired chain shot. This is highly unlikely since this specialist ammunition was for use against rigging to render an enemy vessel unmanageable. A piece of alleged chain shot was said to have been found in the present Haven Inn. However, as previously mentioned, the present inn was not standing in 1784. The alleged shot was in fact made by a local fisherman. As with so many romantic tales it is fiction, like Hookey's Hole. Local smugglers sometimes made up ghost stories to keep people away from their hides. The crypt, tower or graveyard of churches, if they were used to store contraband, for example, would make ideal settings for a ghost story.

The ships' gunfire had been heard in Christchurch and the Riding Officers gathered at Jeans' house for orders. He told them that he was going to bed and his advice was for them to do the same. He instructed them to falsify their journals and not to log the run or the action at Mudeford. The subsequent enquiry arising from the scandal of killing a naval officer revealed Jeans' duplicity; he and Bursey were then dismissed the service in May 1786. Jeans died six months later, aged 64, leaving a family including a daughter who was married to the Vicar of Christchurch. One son was a doctor and another was a clergyman who became chaplain to the British Ambassador to France.

The smuggler Streeter was arrested but broke jail in 1786, by bribery, and escaped to the Channel Isles. He came back to Christchurch from time to time to visit his family, fathered a son there and was eventually buried in the Priory, aged 74, in 1824. As a result of Allen's murder a reward of £200 was offered in February 1785 and three smugglers were later charged: Henry Voss, John Edwards and George Coombes. Others were known but escaped or evaded capture, or evidence was lacking, as with: Guernsey Jimmy, William Burden, Berry, Wibbal, Parrott (father and son), May and Streeter. Only one smuggler was hung for the murder of William Allen, not Captain William Parrott who fired the fatal shot (all engaged were liable), but George Coombes; who was executed on 23rd January 1786 at Execution Dock on the Thames. His body was brought round by sea to be hung in chains at Mudeford Quay. However his friends took the body down on the first night it was there and gave it a decent burial.

1784 continued to be a violent year. In early August another fight took place on the North Shore of Poole Harbour. The *Salisbury Journal* reported ' Scarce a night passes without a skirmish which too frequently terminates fatally to one of the parties, if not both'.

In August 1784 *HMS Hebe*, a frigate, based at Portsmouth, a 40 gun vessel taken from the French in 1782, seized 130 tubs of spirit in a boat west of Portsmouth. On 17th August the cutter *Expedition* was informed that a 32 gun cutter and a 12 gun lugger was expected to make a run at Christchurch Bay. The smuggling cutter had loaded at Ostende with a cargo said to be valued at £27,000 (a vast sum in those days). The smuggling vessel had contracted to land her cargo before 23rd August; hence the contract date was frustrated. The *Expedition* being outgunned sent to *HMS Hebe* for assistance. The *Hebe* sailed east about the Isle of Wight to cut the smugglers off from seaward. The two smuggling craft were discovered off St. Catherine's Point and a running fight took place. *Expedition* lost her top mast and fell behind. The smugglers signalled their surrender, but when the *Hebe* hove to and hoist out her boats, the smugglers sailed off in the dark. Since once *Hebe's* boats were in the water and on their way to take possession she had to recover their crews before she could resume the chase. A journal of the time reported 'The exertion and bravery of the [smuggling] crews were beyond example, and we cannot but lament that such resolution and courage were not employed in better cause'. Later in the month *Hebe* brought into Portsmouth a lugger 'taken on the back of Wight' with 300 casks of spirit.

In September 1784 *HMS Orestes* captured a lugger, the *British Lion*, (24 x 9 and 6 pdr. guns). The lugger fought hard for 40 minutes off Hengistbury Head; only 13 wounded crew members survived to be taken prisoner. After the action in July the crew of the *Orestes* may not have easily granted quarter. The *Orestes* lost two and had nine wounded. The seized lugger was taken to Cowes; she was laden with 13 tons of tea and 6,000 tubs of spirits (approximately 163 tons of illicit cargo). The *Orestes* also took a 200 ton smuggling vessel (armed with 20 x 6 pdr.) after a fight, when a run was attempted at Hurst Spit. That month *HMS Hebe* brought in two luggers from Alderney taken off the Isle of Wight with 280 casks of spirits and 2¾ tons of tea. The *Hebe* then returned to patrol on a Sunday but was back at Spithead on Tuesday with another prize, a 60 ton lugger with 800 tubs and 4 tons of tea, taken off St. Catherine's Point. One of the captured smugglers had been involved in the battle at Mudeford in July.

In October 1784 a wagon load of unlicensed wool was seized near Poole. In December the customs cutter *Rose* made a seizure of spirits and tobacco. Shortly before Christmas customs officers aided by a detachment of 3rd Dragoon Guards seized 120 tubs of spirits and some tobacco near Swanage.

Smuggling tea became unprofitable in 1784 when the duty was reduced from 119% to 12½%. Smugglers then bought duty paid tea and offered it for sale as smuggled! (Also an offence).

In January 1785 a skirmish took place in Westover Lane at Milford Green when smugglers met revenue officers supported by a small party of the South Lancashire Militia from Lymington. The smugglers had 14 wagons and 100 armed horsemen, having landed a run at Hurst Spit. The smugglers consented to give up 100 tubs but offered to open fire if more were sought. Due to the great disparity in numbers the smugglers were permitted to preserve the bulk of their cargo without violence. During the year customs warehouses were again broken into at Poole and the seized goods rescued.

Also in January 1785, *HMS Flirt*, sloop, brought into Cowes a seized lugger and 300 casks of spirits. While *HMS Hebe* sent into Portsmouth a cutter with 300 casks of spirits. Excise men with two dragoons seized a four horse wagon and its load of malt near Southampton, when two or three kegs were found to be concealed in the malt. Vehicles used in keeping, carrying or concealing smuggled goods were liable to seizure, as were the goods used to conceal the contraband. The penalty was loss of the vehicle and cargo as well as the smuggled goods and a fine of three times the duty. Such wagons, horses, cargoes or ships were then put up for public auction. Often only the smugglers would bid and buy them back cheaply.

Still in January 1785, a French smuggling vessel was wrecked on the back of the Isle of Wight. *HMS Hebe* chased the *Amelia,* cutter, of Christchurch, which escaped only after throwing casks of spirit overboard. The *Hebe* recovered 200 half ankers (tubs) and 50 ankers from the sea and brought them into Portsmouth.

In February 1785 the *Swift*, cutter, took a French vessel into Jersey which was found to be laden with brandy, tea, coffee and other duty free goods. Her captain was French but his crew was made up of Scots, Irish and Americans. The following month the customs cutter *Swan* bought 500 tubs into Cowes, her second prize in two weeks, which totalled 5,000 gallons.

In April *HMS Flirt* seized a tub boat and 30 tubs which she took into Portsmouth, and *HMS Hebe* captured the *Happy Return* with 67 casks.

In May the cutter, *Pilot*, seized the vessel *Nancy Limebourne*, with tea and coffee en-route from L'Orient to Amsterdam, and took her prize into Cowes. The same month the cutter, *Pigmy*, captured the cutter *Experiment* laden with tea and brandy. She was also taken into Cowes, as was a lugger with a French crew of only four men, chased and captured by the cutter *Yarmouth*. This prize had only 60 tubs of spirit but it was believed that others had been thrown overboard. Also in May 1785 John How a customs man at Lymington was attacked and severely hurt. The Commissioners awarded him £30 in compensation and £6 for his horse.

In July 1785 a Cherbourg vessel was taken laden with brandy and sent into Cowes. Also at Cowes in July, *HMS Orestes* brought in a large boat laden with 160 casks of spirits and 25 bags of tobacco; and customs cutter *Speedwell* brought in two smuggling vessels with 268 casks of spirits.

In November the *Speedwell* brought into Southampton a lugger with 500 casks of spirits together with coffee and bale goods. That month the mate and a boat's crew of six men from the revenue cutter *Laurel* were captured by 30 smugglers off Alum Chine. The customs men were held prisoner while the run was completed. Also in November *HMS Hebe* took a smuggling sloop laden with geneva and tobacco off the Isle of Wight.

Yarmouth and Battery from the Solent, c. 1855

In December 1785 the *Shark*, revenue cutter, sent into Cowes a large tub boat with 156 casks of spirits. Shortly before Christmas the Collector at Cowes seized the *Fly* from Amsterdam and the *Ceres* from Rotterdam, 'both had an immense quantity of spirits in small casks'.

A Christchurch schoolboy, Richard Warner, at the St. Michael's Loft School from 1786 to 1790, reports of seeing smugglers at work in his Literary Recollections of 1830. The school was in the room above the Lady Chapel at the east end of the Priory, it had extensive views to Hengistbury Head over the Harbour, as can be seen today from the St. Michael's Loft Museum, opened in 1978. (Unfortunately some modern buildings now partly obscure the view). Warner writes ' ...20 or 30 wagons with an armed man at the front of each with 200 or 300 horsemen each with two or four tubs of spirits ....' . A frequent route from Hengistbury Head was to cross the Stour (Wick ferry or ford) and to make to the north east, towards Bransgore and the New Forest. The numbers were usually far too many for the six or so local Riding Officers to take on'. Warner described smugglers as ' ... ruffians, hardened, determined, desperate and generally half-maddened by liquor'.

The route taken by smugglers are sometimes recorded by local road names. Examples could include: Beacon Drive, Highcliffe; Smugglers Lane(s) North (and) South, Highcliffe; Smugglers Wood Road, Highcliffe; Anchor (anker?) Close, Mudeford; Owls ('owlers'?) Road, Boscombe; Beacon Road, West Cliff Bournemouth; Anchor Close, Kinson; Anchor Road, Bear Cross; Owls Road, Verwood; Smugglers Lane, Colehill; Gullivers Court, Wimborne; Kingsmill, Oakdale. More certain names arising from smuggling are: Smugglers Bank at Studland; Brandy Hole in Pitts Deep at Boldre and Brandy Bay adjacent to Kimmeridge Bay. The brandy names probably arise from the sinking of casks of brandy to be recovered later when the coast was clear.

Some substantial country houses were built with the proceeds of smuggling, for example Gulliver's home at Kinson. Other apparently more respectable people may have also had a hand in the trade. Gustav Brander, a successful Swedish timber merchant, built the Priory House in 1777, just south of Christchurch Priory Church in the grounds of the old Monastery, with extensive views over the Harbour. He was responsible for the first ever book on fossils (at Barton) and was wealthy enough to be able to entertain Louis Phillippe, the exiled King of the French, at his home in 1807. In 1792 a John Brander owned a sloop, the *Stour* of 24 tons burden. This vessel, Captain Richard Rogers, carried bricks to Plymouth and Newhaven and freight to Truro and London. Another possible example is Captain Tregonwell of the

South Dorset Yeomanry Cavalry (volunteer force) who had a fine house at Cranborne Chase. He built a property 'for his wife' at a lonely coastal spot at Bourne Bottom, now the Exeter Hotel at Bournemouth. Tregonwell also built a home for Symes, his butler. This was Portman Cottage which was demolished in 1930. When this building was removed it was found to conceal a smuggler's hide, 3 ft below ground, 10ft long, 7 ft wide and 6 ft high.

Smugglers in the Purbeck area were able to use caves, either natural or cut, and also rock piles to conceal goods. In the sand and gravel of Bourne Heath and Christchurch it was necessary to construct or adapt cellars. The local iron pan appears naturally in the gravel and is often wrongly alleged to be a roof of a smuggler's tunnel. Sewers on the site of the monks' quarters at the Priory could have been mistaken for tunnels. The need was for storage cellars, as at the site which became the Fountain Inn, at Christchurch, rather than for tunnels to remote locations. The low altitude of Christchurch and the (then) high water table also gave risk of flooding in cellars and tunnels. One urgent hiding place was provided by ladies fashions. A woman could sit on a tub of spirits and conceal it under her skirts while she bathed or fed a child. This apparently happened at the Eight Bells Inn at Church Street, Christchurch. This inn was named for the seven bells in the Priory peal - like the 19th hole, the Golf club bar. The George and Dragon, The Dolphin, The Hoy (at Highcliffe) and other inns in the same area were also involved in 'the trade'. Local people refer to the inn the St. George and Dragon as 'The George'. This has misled the brewers to label it a century ago as *The George* after a Hanoverian king and to call it 'Ye Olde George Inn'.

Articles in the *Salisbury Journal* and *Hampshire Chronicle* bore reports of the larger local seizures by crown vessels:

January 1786 the *Speedwell*, customs cutter, sent into Cowes a large tub boat with 272 casks of spirit. Later that month the *Swan* sent into the same port three prizes: a cutter with 85 casks and two tub boats, one with 150 tubs the other with 299 tubs. The revenue at Hamble seized 224 kegs of spirit on the shore.

February 1786 the *Rose*, customs cutter, brought into Portsmouth a large vessel from Alderney with 500 ankers and some larger casks of brandy and hollands (gin) and boxes of tea. The whole cargo was worth between £3,000 to £4,000. The Customs Surveyor at Portsmouth seized gold and silver lace with upwards of 3,000 dollars which an East Indiaman was attempting to export. The cutter, *Roebuck*, seized two boats with 100 tubs at Portsmouth.

The Semaphore at the entrance to Portsmouth Harbour
Engraving of a painting by Stanfeld RA, c. 1810.

The *Speedwell* brought into Cowes a large vessel with 300 casks and two tub boats with 381 casks of spirit. Later in the month a warehouse belonging to Poole Custom House was broken open and several casks of spirit stolen. Four labourers confessed to the crime but one of them escaped.

In March 1786 the *Speedwell* brought into Cowes 200 to 300 casks of spirit. The *Resolution*, excise cutter, sent into Cowes a vessel laden with French wines, silks and other goods. The *Rose* brought into Southampton a smuggling vessel and between 200 and 300 kegs of spirit, taken up at sea when the smuggler was chased. Another revenue cutter also took up casks of spirits thrown overboard by the smuggler.

In June of the same year *HMS Hebe* took a large open boat laden with 166 casks of spirit, some tea and wine. The revenue cutter, *Expedition* brought into Cowes a cutter with foreign spirits. In the following month the *Hebe* captured another open boat with 50 cases of liquors.

In October 1786 *HMS Fleet*, sloop, brought into Portsmouth an open boat with 117 casks of spirit. Hence the small open tub boats were prepared to operate in the winter risking bad weather but gaining the benefit of darkness.

Hebe was again at Portsmouth, in November, with a seizure of 250 casks of spirits and 1½ tons of tobacco. A boat from the *Rose* brought into Lymington a tub boat with 100 casks of spirit. In December the *Swan* brought into Cowes a lugger with 600 casks of spirit. The boats of the *Laurel* revenue cutter seized a cutter from Truro in Studland Bay with over 400 tubs of spirits on 28th December.

In January 1787 the *Hebe* made another capture with 400 kegs of spirit taken to Portsmouth and the *Rose* sent into Southampton 150 tubs of spirit and some dry goods. In the same month, excise officers and dragoons made a capture in the New Forest, and the *Speedwell* fired on a French smuggler off Jersey which blew up with the loss of all hands when she received *Speedwell's* second broadside.

In February 1787 *HMS Myrmidon*, frigate, brought into Portsmouth a cutter and a large boat with 370 casks of spirit. Also customs officers at Christ-church supported by a party of dragoons seized 400 casks of spirits onshore at Chewton. They were taken into Christchurch in four wagons and sent from there by sea to Southampton Custom House. Another 400 casks were seized and sent to Cowes. Ankers of spirits were seized at Lymington, where the smugglers attempted a rescue but only carried off a few casks. This seizure was sent to Southampton by sea.

During the following month *HMS Hebe* came into Portsmouth with a cutter laden with 440 casks of spirits and 80 bales of tobacco. In the same week revenue cutters had sent into Southampton 800 casks of spirits. The *Antelope*, revenue cutter, seized 99 casks of spirits near Portsmouth.

In May 1787 *HMS Flirt*, sloop, brought into Portsmouth 200 kegs, and the *Roebuck*, customs cutter, 250 kegs of spirits. The *Rose*, customs cutter, brought into Southampton 300 casks of spirits, tea, wine and tobacco with a boat and six prisoners. The *Enterprise*, excise cutter, brought into Portsmouth the smuggling vessel *Friends*, of Hamble, having on board 120 bales of India silk from Dunkirk. *HMS Orestes*, sloop, made her fifth seizure since the beginning of the year, in May, when she took two schooners off Portland laden with spirits and tobacco. She had a good month, since she subsequently seized a lugger on 24th May, and on 25th May seized two more luggers, all laden with spirits, which were taken into Weymouth.

Also that month, a boat's crew from the *Rose* was involved in an adventure off Christchurch. On 11th May the mate of the *Rose*, with four crew were in a boat about two miles out when at midnight they discovered a sloop making for the shore. They gave chase and boarded the sloop, which had a crew of six men and a boy. The vessel contained casks and other goods and so was seized. However, another smuggling craft came up and the smugglers rescued their cargo. Then in turn another revenue boat came to assist and so the vessel and her cargo was seized and the smugglers were taken prisoner. The smugglers' captain escaped and the six prisoners were sent off to Winchester jail. However, four miles from Lymington the two coaches they were in were stopped by 30 armed, disguised men on horseback who attacked the 12 guards and released the smugglers. It seems that the smugglers' captain had organised a rescue.

In June 1787 the *Lively*, revenue cutter, brought into Southampton the lugger, *Hit or Miss*, with 280 casks of spirit, tobacco, currants, starch, hair powder and soap. At Parkstone, near Poole, two Riding Officers seized three horses and 23 tubs of spirits from smugglers. *HMS Flirt*, sloop, brought 70 casks of spirit into Portsmouth. *HMS Scout*, sloop, brought into the same port a boat with 94 casks of spirits and 7 bags of tea.

HMS Myrmidon brought a large boat with 250 casks into Portsmouth in July and at the same port *HMS Flirt* brought in a similar capture and 160 casks.

In the same month the *Trial*, cutter, took a 14 gun French privateer after an action west of Durlston Head.

In November 1787 there was a violent fracas at the North Shore of Poole Harbour. The boat's crew of a customs cutter fought on-shore with a formidable gang of smugglers. Several of both sides were desperately wounded, but the smugglers carried off their tobacco and other contraband. They were then attacked by other officers assisted by dragoons and a more dreadful conflict ensued; several lives were lost.

An Act was passed in 1787 to permit only Royal Navy and revenue vessels to have cutters with bowsprits more than two-thirds the length of the hull. Cutters had moveable bowsprits capable of adjustment according to the weather, like topmasts. The bowsprits on the other vessels like sloops were fixed, but were able to be lengthened by the use of a jib boom which could be removed in bad weather. Usually a cutter carried two small boats able to be stored on deck. Typically, a cutter was armed with at least eight or more 6 pounder carronades (short range smashers), plus eight swivel guns at bow and stern which could also be used from the ship's boats. From 1788 the Customs Commissioners ceased to hire vessels on contract and relied on their own and naval vessels.

Two excise officers were murdered by smugglers in Devon in 1787 and also in that year there was another fight with smugglers at Bournemouth. A lugger had landed tubs at Bourne Mouth but abandoned them and its two tub boats when the revenue cutter *Resolution* was seen approaching. A boat's crew from the *Resolution* seized the kegs but they were rescued by 30 mounted smugglers. The Mate of the *Resolution*, Mr Quick, ordered the smugglers to disperse and when they refused ordered his men to fire. The smugglers charged, wounding Quick and one of his men, driving the rest of the boat's crew into the surf and rescuing their cargo. As a result, a smuggler was later tried and John Butler, aka Bishop, was hung at Newgate in May 1788.

In February 1788, a wounded smuggler was captured at Christchurch. The man had lost an eye from a pistol shot when fighting with the crew of the *Rose* revenue cutter. He had escaped to Christchurch but must have been informed upon, his wound being obvious. Revenue men in three post chaises (fast coaches) went to Christchurch to apprehend him and take him to Winchester jail. During the same month the customs at Weymouth burnt 70,000 tons of seized tobacco.

said to be mainly Irish. The customs men were ordered on board the lugger but refused, so the lugger got underway and chased the revenue boat, firing on her. At 8pm the following day, a boat from the *Swan* customs cutter fell in with the same lugger near Christchurch. The interference by the *Rose's* boat had clearly frustrated the run at Beckton Bunny. The *Swan's* boat gave chase, but when it came up to her the revenue men were captured and taken on board the lugger which sailed to Bourne Bottom. There, at 2 o'clock in the morning, the lugger landed her goods, some 1,000 casks of spirits, tea and tobacco. The revenue men were then put back in their boat minus their weapons and some boat's stores.

On Christmas Eve 1790 there was a run at Chewton Bunny east of the mansion called High Cliff on the shores of Christchurch Bay. The goods were taken into the New Forest probably via the Cat and Fiddle Inn at Hinton.

In April 1791, Collector Arnold at Cowes reported ' ...smugglers more daring than ever, and more frequently assemble in numbers carrying arms and in disguise ... officers being wounded, beaten, opposed and obstructed...' He could have been influenced by events at Christchurch. On 24th April at 4am, Robert Weeks, Supervisor, and Riding Officers Dale, Dean, Pike and Preston were on duty at Shenfield near Christchurch. (They must clearly have had reason to be together there at that time of night.) They fell in with 30 smugglers, some on horseback, armed with bats (metal-shod staves), who were guarding four carriages loaded with tubs of spirit. Officer Dean was knocked off his horse and violently beaten. Officer Pike was hit on the head. The officers were forcibly detained and threatened with murder if they resisted. Dean was robbed of his pistol and horse.

Work on a cavalry barracks at Christchurch began in 1792, arising from the fourth Report of the Commissioners of Military Enquiry. Initially accommodation was provided for one troop of horse and subsequently for three troops of cavalry or one of Royal Horse Artillery. The South Hampshire Militia were temporarily accommodated at the Kings Arms, Christchurch, before occupying the barracks in 1784. The 20th Light Dragoons were in post by 1795. The barracks were built as an anti-invasion precaution rather than to put down smuggling. By 1797 the Royal Horse Artillery were at the barracks. (F Troop were sent to Ireland the same year to put down rebellion.) Local and other volunteers also probably used the barracks, including : Loyal Christchurch Volunteer Artillery (1794-1808), Christchurch (Sea) Fencible Volunteers (Fishermen), Christchurch Troop South Hampshire Volunteer Yeomanry Cavalry (called Carabineers since armed with carbines), South Hants. Militia (local company). There were also probable visits from: the

Dorset Yeomanry Volunteer Cavalry, Dorset Militia, Kings German Legion (at Lymington from 1803) and French Royalist Units (at Ringwood and Lymington to 1797), Lancashire and Lincoln Militia also used the barracks and had other detachments at Lymington, and other units (dragoons) were at Wimborne and Blandford. The Sea Fencibles (also at Lymington and Poole) were controlled by the Royal Navy, though in some cases they were virtually armed smugglers. In 1803 the 20th Light Dragoons had a troop at Christchurch and later that year C Troop RHA. Different cavalry and RHA troops were at the barracks until the 1860s by which time smuggling was defeated.

Collector Arnold had a series of cutters, called *Swan*, built at Cowes. He had become frustrated by witnessing the construction of vessels for smugglers faster than any revenue ship. The first *Swan* was wrecked on her first voyage and was replaced by *Swan II,* the vessel engaged in the battle at Mudeford. This cutter seized 1,000 or more tubs at Bournemouth in January 1792 but was wrecked that year near Shoreham and was replaced by *Swan III.* In 1793 she captured two French privateers but in 1795 was herself captured by three French frigates. A 34 ton seized cutter, the *Nancy*, was then used until the 120 ton *Swan IV* was built in 1796. She recaptured a sloop from the French but in 1799 was taken after a fight with a large French cruiser and her captain killed. She was recaptured by the Royal Navy in the same year. *Swan V*, 155 tons, was built to replace her but in 1807 was captured by three French luggers six miles off The Needles. Four of her men were captured but 20 escaped in a boat, they were all pressed by the Royal Navy.

In 1794 Jack Rattenbury was running smuggled goods into Beer in Devon coastwise from Christchurch. This indicates that coastal vessels were able to avoid the same level of scrutiny as those from foreign, perhaps due to collusion by Coastal Waiters. At about this time two Devonshire smuggling craft were captured, one taken into Portsmouth, the other into Southampton.

The *Vigilant*, sloop, made a successful run, in 1796, right up Poole Harbour. She anchored off the quay and at night unloaded her tubs of spirits into punts which went up into the shallows of Holes Bay.

In July 1796 the *Rose* revenue cutter took a French privateer lugger about half-way across the Channel. The *Rose* only had 16 men aboard, the rest away in her boats. The lugger had a crew of 36. The prize was taken into Swanage Bay.

First Rate Ships of the Line off The Needles
H. W. Affrey 1858.

On 29th August that year Samuel Hookey, a Christchurch smuggler, was supposed to be drowned in the Stour at the age of 71 while fleeing revenue men. He may have been wearing a money belt of sovereigns for use in a guinea boat. Gold was being sought in Hookey's Hole in the Stour as late as 1954. Unfortunately the story of Sam Hookey's death at Hookey's Hole is an invention. Mr R. Ede England of The Lawn, Mudeford created the yarn to justify 'Hookey's Bar' at a local resort. The evidence is a letter dated 26th February 1962 sent to the curator of the Red House Museum by Mr Ede England. It is not unknown for other local 'watering holes' to be named for non-existent smuggling events or personalities. So unnecessary when the area abounds in the history of the real thing.

In February 1797 the French attempted a raid in force as a preliminary to invasion. They loaded 1,400 men into three frigates and two luggers, and aimed to attack near Bristol and draw off troops from south-east England. They first went into the Bristol Channel and sank some coastal shipping at Ilfracombe. They were fired on from the shore and so decided to try elsewhere. They landed at Fishguard in Wales where they were resisted by a small scratch force made up of Sea Fencibles (local fishermen), local gentry and farm workers, a few RN sailors at Fishguard Harbour, and the crews of revenue cutters *Diligence* and *Speediwell* who landed their guns and moved them 27 miles across country on carts. The main resistance was organised by the Castlemartin Yeomanry Cavalry (later the Pembroke Yeomanry) a widely scattered volunteer corps, (like the South Hants. and the Dorset Volunteer Yeomanry Cavalry). The French outnumbered their opponents two to one. However, the red cloaks of Welsh women on the hills and the arrival of the customs cutters guns convinced them that they were facing a regular army of infantry, cavalry and artillery, so they surrendered unconditionally. The *Vautour* one of the French vessels, a lugger, was returning to Brest when she was chased for eight hours by the revenue cutter *Greyhound.* She was taken only nine miles from her home port and was brought as a prize into Weymouth. In 1801 the *Greyhound* of Weymouth was handed over to the Royal Navy with the cutters *Rose* and *Antelope* of Southampton. They were sent to The Downs to join Nelson's anti-invasion flotilla.

In June 1797 the sloop *Betsey* of Poole was taken but recaptured from the French by the revenue cutter *Hind.* In July the *Trial*, cutter, took a 14 gun French privateer off Portland. At about this time it is said that a woman informer at Barton-on-Sea was murdered by smugglers. She was asphyxiated as she slept because the chimney, windows and door sills of her cottage had been blocked with damp blankets. There were several affrays at Barton between revenue men and the Black Gang of smugglers. Another gang was the Ambrose Hole Gang of Lymington, who were also burglars. They are alleged to be responsible for 30 murders, putting the bodies in a well. The mud flats at Lymington enabled tubs to be off-loaded into wild-fowler punts where no other boat could go. Once a Riding Officer had to call out the dragoons before he could saw in half and burn an unlicensed galley found building in a lonely Bunny.

The following year the sloop, *HMS Wasp*, searched a suspect vessel and found a letter to John Early of Christchurch, a known smuggler. The letter, from a senior customs officer at Poole, contained details of military dispositions in the Poole area. The writer, a man named Weston, was dismissed from the service.

The Parkstone Riding Officer was attacked by three smugglers in 1799. A few years later the Riding Officer at Milford had his saddle girths cut. Also during 1799, another officer 'fell over a cliff' at Branscombe in Devon and a customs boatman was shot dead at Lymington. He lies in the same grave-yard as a smuggler who died of wounds in action with the revenue cutter *Rose*. Also in that year the *Bee,* cutter, was wrecked in Studland Bay. A Royal Humane Society medal was awarded to the owner of Brownsea who led a daring rescue by boat.

On one occasion revenue men with a knowledge of a run hid themselves in shallow trenches in the beach above the high tide line, each man covered by seaweed. The ambush, in the Friars Cliff area was successful and the seized goods sent to Poole by wagon via Iford. The wagoners got drunk on the brandy and so the horses turned around and took the easier route, back to Christchurch, rather than pull up the hill to Pokesdown (Puck's Hill).

A smuggler at Bembridge, named Dawes, had an attractive daughter, Sophie. She and her brother had been put in the Poor House when children but as a teenager she was involved in smuggling. There is a story (almost certainly false) that while dressed in men's clothes she was captured on land on the Isle of Wight and the young naval officer concerned recognised her as female. He was a younger brother of the diplomat who later built the second High Cliff mansion (miscalled Castle). She did not stay long at John Stuart's mother's home at Bure and was packed off to London and passed on to another young man who subsequently lost her in a card game. It is known that she worked as a servant in a London brothel and that she ended up in France, as the mistress of the Duc de Bourbon, last Prince de Condè, and in 1818 became the Baroness de Feucheres. (She was later suspected of having murdered her husband). Later in life she returned to England and built Bure Homage, a mansion at Friars Cliff which was demolished in 1957.

Another female, but one who remained at the lower end of the social scale was Lovey Warne. She lived at Knave's Ash, Crow near Burley. She was known for smuggling at Christchurch and Mudeford Quays by wrapping goods like silk or lace around her body under her clothes. She also smuggled liquor in bladders under her clothes. Her red cloak was used as a signal for smugglers.

In February 1803 a Riding Officer from Christchurch seized a wagon with 70 tubs at Shirley, in the Avon Valley north of Mudeford. However, he was attacked and the goods were rescued by smugglers. The next day the wagon concerned was identified at Kinson and was again seized. It was taken for security into the barracks of the 20th Light Dragoons at Christchurch. In April officers at Branksome seized two wagons and a cart with 250 tubs of spirit, some tobacco and a case of playing cards. They were taken to the Custom House at Poole.

In September the *Speedwell*, an 80 ton cutter, ran 300 to 400 tubs into the New Forest from The Beacon at Highcliffe. The run was reported by the *Batt*, revenue cutter, but the Riding Officers found nothing. In the following month, Abraham Pike, the Supervisor of the Riding Officers at Christchurch together with his Riding Officers: Bacon, Newman and Wise, with Mr Buck, Land Waiter, and a customs boats crew; supported by a party from the 20th Light Dragoons seized 63 tubs and a cask of tobacco at Bourne, and subsequently near Kinson two cases of cordial and one of spirits. The rest of the run escaped them.

In December the Riding Officer at Wareham wrote to the Collector at Poole '...companies of smugglers frequent this coast in a very daring manner'. During the year the Collector complained about customs weapons at Poole as ' few old muskets and cutlasses ... useless and cannot be repaired'.

That year, 1803, Poole landed 26 cargoes and shipped 25, mostly to Portsmouth. Christchurch landed 62 and shipped 66 probably smaller cargoes; 22 from and 40 to Portsmouth. Such coastwise trade was in items such as beer, malt, barley, wheat, biscuits, rushes and beech planks, mostly destined for the Royal Navy at Portsmouth. Coal and stone were imported from Newcastle and Portland. The coastal trader *Dove* took freight and passengers from Christchurch to London.

Rigging out a smuggler.

By kind permission of the National Maritime Museum, Greenwich, London.

In 1804 the Poole Collector reported that spirits, wine, tobacco and salt were being run from the Channel Isles. In the summer small tub boats carried 100 to 400 four to six gallon casks. In the winter, vessels of 30 to 130 tons carried 400 to 800 such casks. Boats were making two trips a week or three trips a fortnight. The Collector estimated that 80,000 gallons of spirits were run between Poole and Hengistbury Head each year, the goods being taken into the New Forest. That year the excise cutter *Duke of York* seized goods off Boscombe. Also in 1804 there was a scrimmage with smugglers at Sopley. It was reported in October that, 'the smuggler is got so daring and impudent that they will not give up their goods' when officers attempt a seizure'. German (King's German Legion) troops at Wareham refused to assist revenue officers. In December four revenue men were drowned when a boat from a lugger capsized on Christchurch Ledge.

In the year of Trafalgar, 1805, British customs were stationed on the Channel Isles, which has its own rates of duty. This arrangement also improved customs intelligence on smugglers and their vessels. However, in November 1806 it was reported that 'smuggling has greatly increased'. In the previous month customs officers sought assistance from the 14th Light Dragoons at Wareham but were refused. That month a wagon load of wool, with its horses and the wagon, were seized for being within five miles of the coast without a licence. In September the *Dove* bought a seized lugger from Plymouth to Poole, the cargo was found to be 28 gallons of brandy and 10 gallons of wine short, because of casks being spiled (secretly bored and then plugged, often under a hoop). Also during that month a member of the crew of the *Seagull*, a revenue cutter, was pressed by the Royal Navy when visiting relatives while on leave.

A wagon loaded with wool was seized near Poole in October 1806 by Riding Officers. The wool was valued at £250, the wagon £20 and the horse £48. These were considerable sums of money at the time.

In August 1810 a French prisoner of war, Captain Angerard, a sea officer, made a daring escape from Poole. He had been held at Andover where he and his colleague, Captain Chevallier of a dragoon regiment each purchased a pair of double barrelled pistols from a merchant. A friendly English lady provided a carriage which they rode to Poole, (probably a breach of parole). They put up in a large hotel near the quay but then travelled to Christchurch, staying at The George. They saw a large number of fishing boats in the harbour. However, the hotel landlord had recognised them as Frenchmen but being French himself did not give them away on condition that they did not steal a boat at Christchurch. They walked back to Poole but were challenged by two gentlemen on the way. A fight ensued in which Chevallier received wounds which were to prove fatal. However the prisoners overcame their assailants and reached Poole at 11 o'clock at night. They got into a boat and gained the deck of a revenue cutter which was empty of crew, but ready to be commissioned the next day. They got underway and passed an RN brig in the harbour which did not challenge them. However, at 7am the next day they were chased by another brig but got away by going up the Solent. The following three days were calm, but with a breeze on their fifth day at sea they were chased by a frigate which they outran and reached the Normandy coast. Four days later Chevallier died of internal injuries. Angerard and the family of his late colleague each received one third of the value of the revenue cutter as prize money. The initiative of the Frenchmen only succeeded due to the aid they received from the English lady and the landlord of The George and also because they could speak English and had money to pay their way .

The growth in smuggling was encouraged by the rates of duty and number of items subject to duty. In 1760 some 800 products were liable to duty but by 1810 the number had grown to 2,100 items. Smuggling in the area of what became Bournemouth was an open secret with the local gentry, who connived at it since they were customers, and sometimes financiers, of the smugglers.

A drawing of 1814 shows Bourne Bottom and has the caption " Bourneist's motto 'Spirits of the Deep Arise'", as a pun on smuggling, and drawing out of the sea kegs of spirit sunk for later retrieval by grapnels. This was the process known as creeping, rowing along with grapnels out to drag up tubs which had been deliberately sunk.

To avoid being captured with tubs on board, smuggling vessels took to casting tubs over the side, linked together to be trawled up again later by small boats. The method was to load tubs with rope slings in place and secure them to a drift line. Between each tub hung a stone attached to the drift line to act as a sinker. The anchor was bent to either end of the line to keep the tubs from drifting below the surface. The smuggling vessel slipped off the tubs on given bearings so as to aid recovery. Often, the smugglers would mingle amid fishing boats at dusk to conceal their actions. Later the sunken tubs would be dredged up by a row boat perhaps posing as a crab or lobster boat. The contents of any tubs which leaked or otherwise became polluted were known as 'stinkibus'. An unpopular task for coastguards and revenue boats crew was to row along the shore creeping for tubs. In the winter this could involve working all through the sixteen hours of darkness.

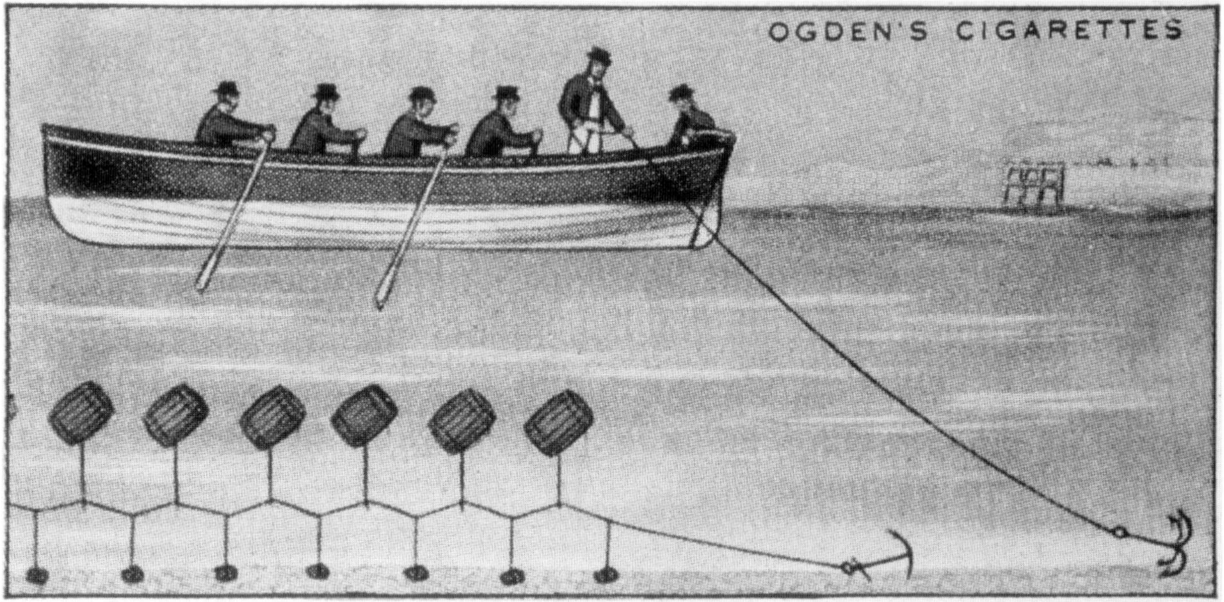

Creeping for tubs
By kind permission of the Board of Trustees of the National Museums and Galleries.
(H.M. Customs and Excise National Museum)

In 1810 a uniformed Customs Waterguard was proposed. The Waterguard operated customs vessels until titles changed in 1972. Initially their service was only in the Thames Estuary and the coasts of Kent and Sussex, but was later extended to cover all coasts. In 1816 they were known as the Preventive Waterguard when the RN was free of war with France, and in 1822 the Coastguard was set up. This eventually (in 1845) comprised a naval reserve of trained men for the fleet, who in peacetime were used to patrol the coasts and prevent smuggling. Between 1821 and 1824 five of these officers were killed and 30 seriously wounded. The new arrangements required that the Riding Officers became a Mounted Guard of ex-cavalrymen; with revenue cruisers, and Preventive Waterguard, all to be administered by the Board of Customs Commissioners.

Smith in his history of the Customs and Excise, '*Something to declare*', has pointed out that 'smuggling was a major crime conducted on a colossal scale, the execution of which was violent, ruthless and bloody in the extreme, even when judged by the brutal standards of the time. The smugglers were encouraged and financed by the local gentry, protected by compliant magistrates, condoned by the clergy, aided and abetted by the ordinary people and at times facilitated by venal revenue officers'.

Well organised and highly disciplined Royal Navy Preventive Service Coastguards eventually got the better of the smugglers. In 1817 the RN began to use blockade techniques on the English Channel coast. Smugglers were forced even more to use small dark beaches, dark nights and stormy dangerous weather. A favourite time was the dark of the moon, the three days either side of the new moon.

Originally, smugglers had relied on the limited number of revenue men and their few ships. As the rewards of smuggling grew the numbers engaged in the trade increased. And slowly the reactions of the revenue service increased following behind the initiatives of the smugglers:

> Use of large gangs armed with staves to overawe the revenue and local people.
> Bribe and/or terrify witnesses and/or jurymen.
> Suborn magistrates.
> Run cargoes ashore on beaches at night with transport ready to remove the goods rapidly inland.
> Conceal dutiable goods in duty free cargoes.
> Use large disciplined gangs with firearms ready to remove the goods rapidly inland.

Carry out fraud by undervaluing goods for duty.
Carry out fraud by claiming goods to be damaged and hence not liable to duty.
Carry out fraud by drawing back duty at export on duty paid goods but relanding the goods duty free.
Obtain duty free goods at sea e.g. from East Indiamen.
Conceal dutiable goods under duty paid or duty free goods, or by under reporting the size and/or value of the cargo.
Conceal smuggled goods in false bottoms and bulkheads, or even in hollow spars.
Tow smuggled goods in watertight casks weighted to float underwater.
Anchor smuggled goods off shore in weighted kegs to be dredged up later when the coast clear.

(From time to time these methods are still attempted).

A Christchurch smuggler named Abe Coakes had a reputation for swimming up The Run at Mudeford on an incoming tide, guiding a line of nearly sub-merged tubs. This would only have been possible on dark nights since the Coastguard occupied cottages at the Haven in 1823.

Smuggling did not give way quickly. In June 1816 the Lymington customs officers seized a boat at Hurst with 127 tubs of spirit and three days later a further six tubs.

Lymington was in such a shift that in 1820 the magistrates swore in the worst of the smugglers as Special Constables to try to ensure order. In that year it is said some 500 smugglers were at Bourne Bottom where they were attacked by revenue officers, and a party of dragoons who seized much of the run. The following year 130 tubs were seized on the beach, where they had been landed and left for collection. The same thing happened in 1822 when 42 tubs were seized, the rest having been removed. Captain Marryat RN, who was posted to coastguard duties, reported in 1822 that probably only one tub in ten was being intercepted. Marryat wrote the *Children of the New Forest* in 1847 when he returned to the area. He is remembered at the Chewton Glen Hotel just east of Chewton Bunny, Hampshire by the use of his name within the hotel. (He is known to have stayed in the house which was owned by his brother.)

The grip of the Coastguard gradually tightened. Eventually there were coastguards stationed all along the coast at: Studland; Brownsea; Poole

Quay; Watch Vessel at Poole Harbour entrance at South Haven until 1876 when a new Coastguard building replaced it at Sandbanks; Flaghead Chine; West Cliff, Bournemouth; Southbourne (Rocket Store) north of White Pitts on the cliffs; Tuckton; Hengistbury Head (Watch House); Stanpit (Fisherman's Bank); Mudeford (Dutch Cottages); Steamer Point (Watch Vessel); Barton-on-Sea (cottages) and so on to Milford; Hurst Castle; Keyhaven and Lymington. The Stanpit location was built in 1861 with a coastguard officer's house, 10 coastguard cottages, boat store house, store, watch room and office. The Royal Navy was better organised and funded than the Customs service. A portable boathouse was at Mudeford in 1869.

In 1820 the cutter *Levant* of Chichester was found to have a double bottom to conceal contraband. On 14th January 1823 the smuggling vessel *Mary* foundered off Christchurch at night. The Coastguard later recovered 80 casks of brandy which drifted ashore from the wreck.

Smuggling did not die out easily. The *Salisbury and Winchester Journal* reported the following events in 1824:

'January, Mr Young, Riding Officer at Bourne Station seized 78 casks of spirits and a boat on the North Shore.
February, Mr Martin, creeped up 89 casks of spirits and one cask of tea off Boscombe.
July, Mr Martin, Chief Officer of Brownsea Station, seized 93 casks of spirits found floating in the sea. (The casks had probably been sunken and had broken adrift from anchors before they had been recovered by smugglers.)
July, Lt. Umfreville RN, of a Coastguard Station seized the yacht *Phoedra* with 66 packages of tobacco and 6 lb. tea.
October, Lt. Elwin RN of Brownsea Coastguard Station creeped up 101 casks of spirits.
November, Lt. Elwin RN, seized 97 casks of spirits on Sandbanks. Mr Brown, Riding Officer seized 13 casks of spirits.'

The Lloyds Insurance Market paid for a lifeboat to be stationed at Christchurch in 1802, but it does not appear to have been stationed there for long. On 8th March 1824 the first ever Royal National Lifeboat Institution Gold Medal award for bravery was won by a coastguard officer Lt. Cmdr. C. Freemantle RN (later an Admiral), who was in command of the detachments from Lymington to the county boundary i.e. inclusive of Christchurch, was at White Pitts near Christchurch. The Swedish brig *Carl Jean* had lost her mast and grounded on the sand bar at Mudeford. Freemantle swam out to the vessel with a rope to rig a lifeline. However the crew refused to use it in the rough seas. Freemantle was pulled ashore in a half-drowned condition by the coastguards using the line. The vessel broke up and the crew got ashore clinging to the broken mast.

On November 23rd 1820, the 100 ton *Hero* was lost off Hengistbury Head with a cargo of stone from Swanage. The following January the Christchurch vessel *Lark* was wrecked off Brownsea and the coastguard saved two men. A coal hoy, *Pilot*, was lost on Boxing Day 1842 en-route to Christchurch.

Another RN officer, Lt. Pym RN, won an RNLI gold medal when the Christchurch vessel *Harm* became a casualty at Whitby in 1848. An RNLI silver medal was awarded to Lt. Parsons RN, who with four Bournemouth coastguards rescued the crew of the Poole barque *William Glen Andison*, when homeward bound from Quebec. She went ashore at Boscombe. The *Christchurch Times* of 15th October 1870 reports the first services of a new lifeboat. (Whether Lloyds, RNLI or other financier's is in question.) The RNLI stationed an inshore lifeboat at Mudeford in 1963. However, Ken Derham had been operating a rescue boat from Avon Beach from 1936. He was awarded the RNLI silver medal in 1959.

In 1824 tubs of spirit were found floating off Boscombe having broken away from their mooring. The Coastguard crept for casks and recovered 89 in all. Brandy which had been polluted with sea water was often not potable. However, if not too polluted the brandy could be drunk with the addition of lovage, an alcoholic cordial. Also in the same year a Coastguard rowboat creeping along with grapnels out raised tubs in Studland Bay. In July the Christchurch preventive boat arrested the 14 ton *Phaedra* in the Harbour with 660 lb. of tobacco and 6 lb. of tea concealed under a false deck.

Three coastguards were attacked by 70 to 80 smugglers at Lyme Regis, in 1825. The mob attempted to cut the throat of one man and stoned the others from the cliff tops. Later in the year Dr Quartley of Bridge Street, Christchurch, operated on a smuggler for a gunshot wound. The man died three days later at Milton. Also in 1825 the entire crew of *Rose*, revenue cutter, were dismissed for seeking to run tobacco.

The following year a Portland smuggler wounded a revenue man at Church Ope Cove, as a result he was sentenced to death, commuted to two years imprisonment. Also in 1826, Dr Quartley wrote in his diary of being taken from his house to cut a slug from a wounded smuggler at Bransgore and being rewarded with a tub of brandy. Years later the man identified himself to the doctor when rowing him on the Avon.

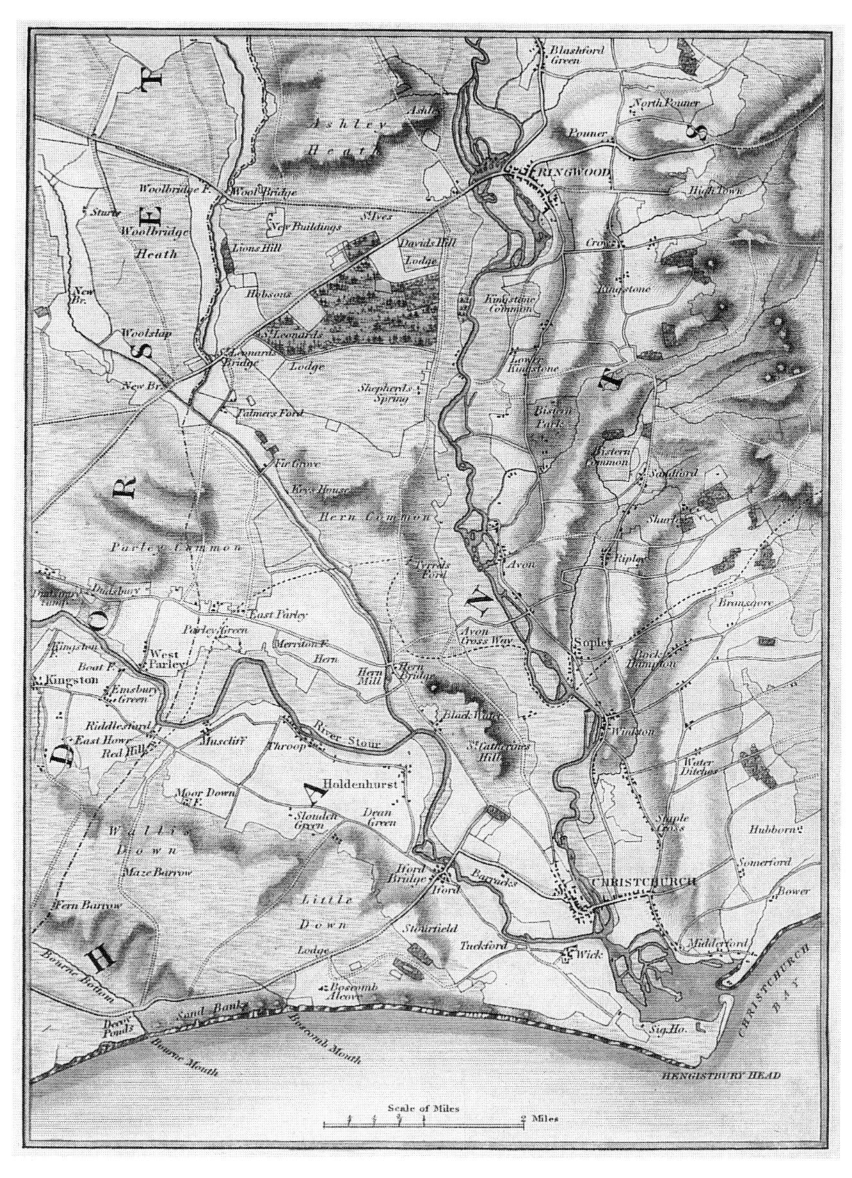

The Environs of Christchurch, c. 1820
(Showing Kingston [Kinson], Hern [Hurn] and Bower [Bure])

In 1826 two luggers the *Fox* and *Lively Lass* of Portsmouth were found to have kegs of spirits in a temporary casing made under the ship's bottom. A similar hide was found on the *Daniel and William* of Portsmouth, a well-known smuggling vessel. This ship had a set of sails of different cut and colour to lend her a disguise.

During the following year two luggers beached themselves below St. Aldhelm's Head in order to run their cargoes ashore. The 80 smugglers employed were attacked by 10 coastguards who killed two and wounded several. The following day more of the smugglers were captured and part of their run was seized. Also in 1827 the *Industry* of Cowes was found towing sunken tubs. The Coastguard Lieutenant at Lulworth was dismissed for not reporting a run; not attempting a seizure; withdrawal of patrol and consorting with smugglers. There were similar cases in Cornwall, Devon and Norfolk. The replacement Lieutenant at Lulworth was murdered by being thrown over the cliff by smugglers. Two coastguards were similarly murdered in the 1830s. It was reported that in 1830 a revenue man was beaten by smugglers at Melcombe Regis and robbed of his weapons. Up to 1830 it was estimated that there were 30 smuggling gangs working between Purbeck and Hengistbury Head.

In 1829 a raft of tubs with a lantern was found floating up Langston Harbour on the tide. Stealth rather than violence was being used. However, in the period before Christmas 1831, two Weymouth smugglers were killed by coastguards when two coastguards and an RN boat's crew fought 100 smugglers. One coastguard was badly wounded and only 66 tubs were seized. The smugglers used swingles, iron-shod flails, which were able to strike an opponent over his cutlass guard. Nevertheless the strict control by the Coastguard was winning the war since in 1831 the Royal Navy was able to lift its anti-smuggling blockade.

Between 1825 and 1840 a tub of brandy cost 16/- to 18/- in France and about £1 in expenses to smuggle. A half-anker tub holds about 4¼ gallons and weighs under 56 lb. Duty paid on a gallon of spirits cost some 36/- in England, hence the gross profit was 32/-. Net profit on a tub was therefore at least £5. 6/-. Also the supplier in France gave 21 tubs to the score, plus two more tubs per 100, to allow for scorage (damages and loss in transit). Spirits could be well over-proof and hence able to be increased in volume by the addition of water. Also burnt sugar was sometimes added to give the spirit colour.

A galley could leave Cherbourg at dusk to sink tubs offshore before dawn. In the 1830s French owned galley operators paid English crewmen £1 for each such trip.

In January 1832 the Chief Officer of Poole Coastguard was dismissed for permitting a vessel to go up the harbour without examination, although he had been informed she had a false bottom. In July the *Mary Anne* of Poole smuggled 600 out of 800 tubs before discovery. The *Captain*, a Portsmouth craft, was found to have a half deck made double to conceal silk goods. In October of the same year F. Fookes, a smuggler aged 17 from East Lulworth was shot while engaged in a run. He was buried at Milton.

In 1833 a raft of 63 tubs with 7ft draught was found in Langston Harbour. Two years later another raft was found there designed to be weighted and so to float below the surface on the incoming tide. No doubt others got through without detection.

In 1835 the *Ant*, a pilot vessel of Cowes was found to have concealment in the bilges. The same year the *Emulation* of Cowes was found to have concealment under her ballast, for 108 tubs and 56 flagons of spirit and some tea. In 1835 the vessel *Mary Anne* of Poole was seized when 800 tubs were discovered under a cargo of coal. Tubs were also concealed on the shore under seaweed, inland under manure heaps, even in a hearse. It was reported that on Christmas Day in 1836 coastguards were in a battle with smugglers at Totland Bay, Isle of Wight, but this was not now so common. By the 1840s the smugglers' use of violence was defeated. The Royal Navy numbers, discipline and weapons had broken them, but the deaths of revenue men continued and so did smuggling.

In 1838 a weighted raft was found in Poole Harbour designed to float up on the tide but below the surface. A similar weighted raft was found in Portsmouth Harbour in 1845. The system was clearly in widespread use. Some got through though and in June 1839 a horse and cart with 20 tubs of spirit were seized at Poole.

In July 1840 a smuggler was fined two shillings for smuggling 4½ lb. of tobacco. He chose to go to prison rather than pay the fine. The arresting customs officer received a reward of 10/- for the conviction and 3 shillings 1¼ d a pound weight for the tobacco.

Coastguards at Hurst captured six smugglers and their boat laden with tubs of brandy in 1848. Five of the smugglers were Frenchmen.

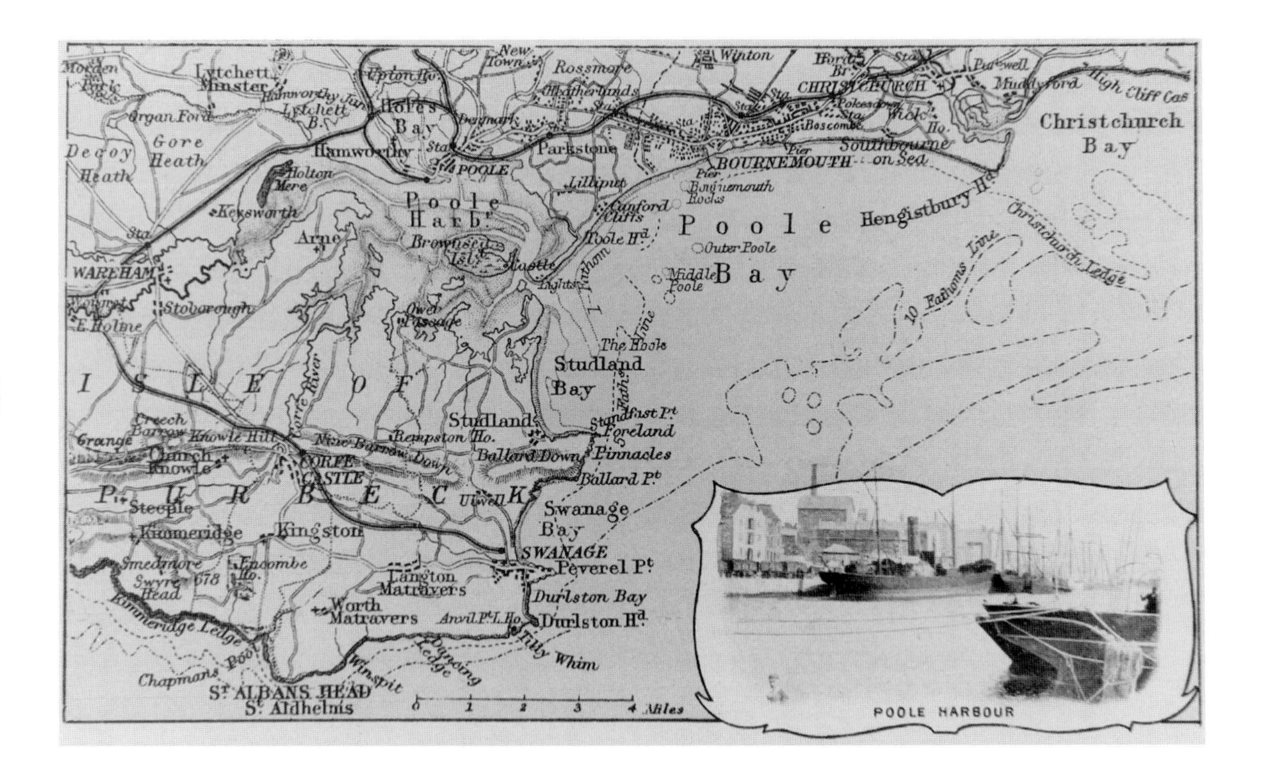

Map of Poole Harbour and Bay c. 1900

In 1859 a coastguard was killed at Haven Quay (Mudeford) by the accidental discharge of a duck gun. In 1861 a civilian died in a shooting accident at Double Dykes and in the following year a punt gun accident at Tuckton narrowly missed an officer and blew off the bows of the punt. Although the smugglers were no longer so predictably violent the unforgiving nature of the sea had not changed and is demonstrated by the 12 drownings on 11th February 1866 from the wrecks off Mudeford and Western Shore (Southbourne).

The author's mother's maternal grandfather, Lt. Dollimore RN, was in the Coastguard service. He had joined the Channel Fleet, aged 14, in 1854 when it was still sail-driven and rose to commissioned rank. His wife had their 17 children in coastguard houses in coastal places like Hull, Leigh-on-Sea and Margate (no knowledge of contraception then), her own mother was one of 21 children! Lt. Dollimore RN held a Royal Humane Society Medal for saving life at sea.

Smuggling gave way slowly. In 1860 the whole population of the shores of the Isle of Wight were described as smugglers. Years later there were reports of smuggling activities. In 1868 seventy two tubs were landed near Yarmouth and 150 tubs were found near Cowes. In 1874 seventeen casks were found near Freshwater.

Smuggling continued at Southampton. In 1871 the cutter *Sunrise* was found in the Itchen with 8,000 lb. of tobacco. The first customs steam launch was stationed at Southampton in April 1872.

The last tub of spirits run into Christchurch (that we know of) was on Christmas Eve 1876. The tub was carried under vegetables in a cart from Lymington. It was for private use at Purewell and was discovered by revenue men searching for a still when the householder was seen to be drunk. A seizure of a still was made in 1942 at Chewton Bunny. A householder had been making the 'hooch' which he sold at £1 a bottle. He was fined £120. So if locals could not smuggle spirits, due to the customs, or due to war, it appears they made their own.

Smuggling, of course, continues to this day. No one is much concerned about the holiday-makers who bring home an extra bottle of duty free. It is the commercial smuggler who is the problem. Often the attention of the revenue can be drawn to offences by complaints from legitimate traders unable to compete with smugglers' prices. Sometimes information is provided by people close to smugglers and sometimes information is shared with the customs services of other countries; sometimes information is obtained by covert means, including electronically.

The greatest challenge to the Customs service in these later years of the twentieth century is from drug and illegal immigrant smuggling, although tax differences between Britain and the Continent mean that tobacco and alcohol smuggling for resale are again reaching serious proportions. The risks are greater than ever: from small yachts and high speed power boats at beaches (Poole and Christchurch Bays) and small harbours (like Christchurch and Lymington); and from cargo and ferry vessels (as at Poole and Southampton). There is also a very substantial risk from aircraft, whether light aircraft on small fields, or commercial flights as at Hurn Airport. The growth of foreign travel, for business or pleasure, has made the customs officers' task even more difficult. The sheer volume of traffic and people create substantial problems. The Customs and Excise have needed to develop appropriate techniques. Drug barons are able to finance people to carry dangerous drugs inside their bodies to avoid detection. The revenue remains vigilant, the curse of hard drugs means that the smuggler is still no gentleman.

Mudeford Quay, nearly cut off by the tide c. 1900

BIBLIOGRAPHY

The author is grateful for information from the following sources:

Christchurch Local History Society, extracts from the ***Salisbury and Winchester Journal*** and from the ***Hampshire Chronicle*** of the late eighteenth century.
K. Merle Chacksfield, **Smuggling Days**; Dorset Publishing, Sherborne 1984.
D. Cross, **The Economic Geography of the Hampshire Basin**; a thesis for an MA degree, reported in the Christchurch Times.
G. Dear, **The Contraband Trade of Christchurch**, Bournemouth Education Committee Leaflet 128, 1972.
R. Guttridge, **Dorset Smugglers**; Dorset Publishing, Sherborne 1984.*
C.R. Hardy, **The Smugglers Guide to Purbeck**; published by the author.
A.D. Hippisley-Coxe, **Smuggling in the West Country**; Tabb House, Padstow 1984.
E. Hathaway, **Smuggler, John Rattenbury**; Shinglepicker Publications, Swanage 1994.
M.A. Hodges, **Prepared for Battle**; published by the author 1982.
R.J. Hutchings, **Smugglers of the Isle of Wight**; Isle of Wight Press, Newport 1990.
G. Hutton and E. Baird, **The Scarecrow's Legion**; Rochester Press 1983.
J. James, **Hurst Castle**; Dovecote Press, Wimborne, 1986.
E.F.J. Mathews, **Gallant Neighbours**; J. Looker, Poole 1934.
G. Morley, **Smuggling in Hampshire and Dorset 1700-1850**; Countryside Books, Newbury 1983.*
G. Morley, **The Smuggling War**; A. Sutton Publishing, Stroud 1994.*
R. Platt, **The Ordnance Survey Guide to Smugglers' Britain**, 1991.
L. Popplewell, **Coastguard and Preventive upon the Shipwreck Coast;** Melledgen Press, Bournemouth 1990.
M.F. Powell and J.E. Clark, **Trade and Smuggling in Christchurch**, 1982.
M.F. Powell, **Christchurch Harbour**; Natula Publications, Christchurch 1995.*
M.F. Powell, **1784 The Battle of Mudeford**; Natula Publications, Christchurch 1993.*
E. Russell Oakley, **The Smugglers of Christchurch, Bournemouth and the New Forest;** Hutchinson, London 1942.
Lt. The Hon. H.N. Shore RN, **Smuggling Days and Smuggling Ways**; Cassell, London 1872.*
B.C. Short, **Smugglers of Poole and Bournemouth**; Dorset Publishing, Bournemouth 1969.

G. Smith, **Something to Declare**; Harrup, London 1980.
G. Smith, **The Kings Cutters, The Revenue Service and the War against Smuggling**; Conway Maritime Press, London 1983.*
G. Smith, **Smuggling in the Bristol Channel 1700-1850**; Countryside Books, Newbury 1989.
M. Waugh, **Smuggling in Devon and Cornwall 1700-1850**; Countryside Books, Newbury 1991.
A. White, **Out of Poole and the Solent Ports 1778-97**; a chart of Maritime history, published by the author 1973.*
A. White, **18th Century Smuggling in Christchurch**; published by the author 1973.*
B.D. Williamson, **Mariners of Ancient Wessex**; published by the author 1998.

* recommended for Christchurch history reading.

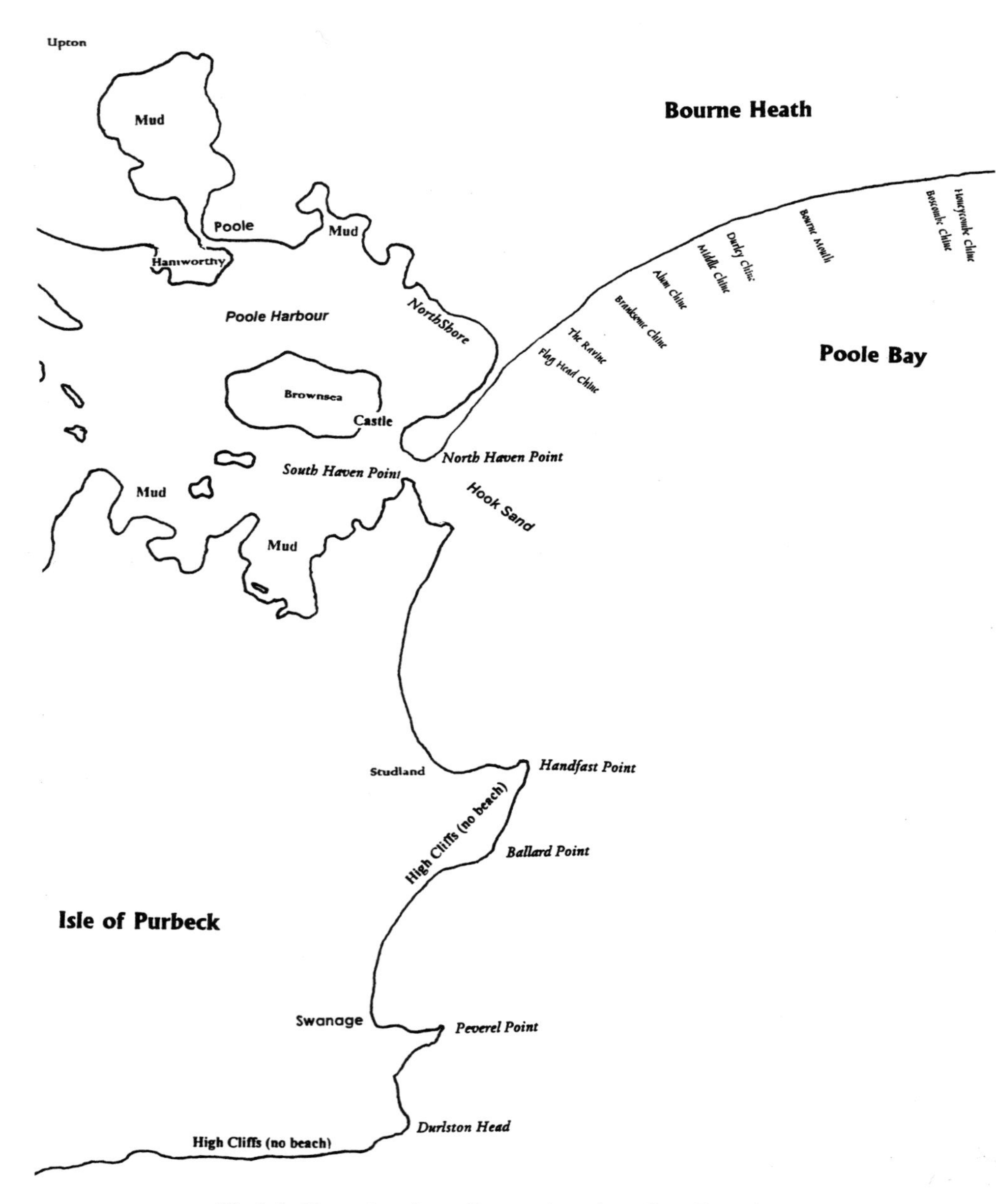

Sketch Maps to show Smugglers Landing Beaches
1. Poole Harbour and Bay

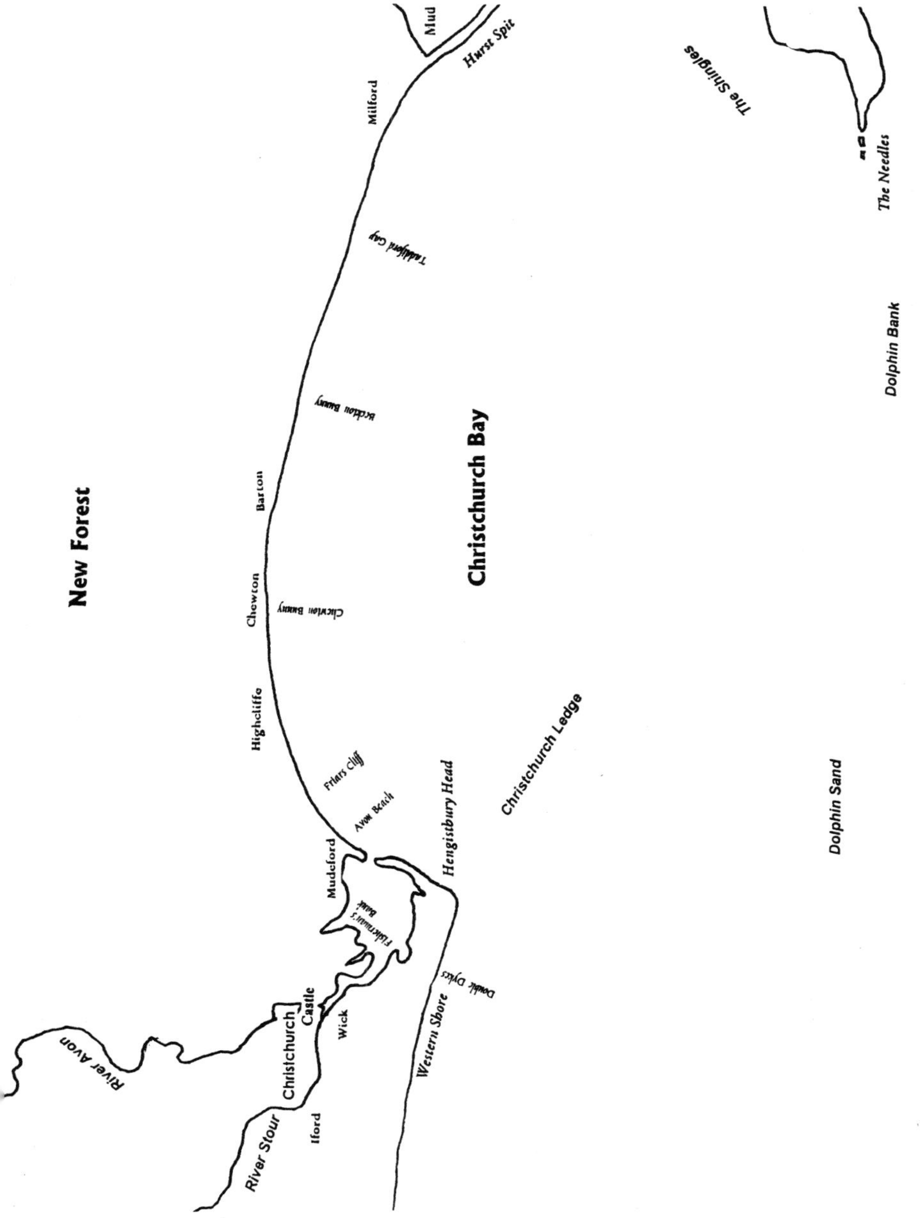

2. Christchurch Bay

New Forest
Christchurch Bay
River Avon
River Stour
Christchurch
Castle
Wick
Iford
Mudeford
Fisherman's Bank
Avon Beach
Friars Cliff
Highcliffe
Chewton
Chewton Bunny
Barton
Beckton Bunny
Taddiford Gap
Milford
Mud
Hurst Spit
The Shingles
The Needles
Dolphin Bank
Dolphin Sand
Christchurch Ledge
Hengistbury Head
Double Dykes
Western Shore

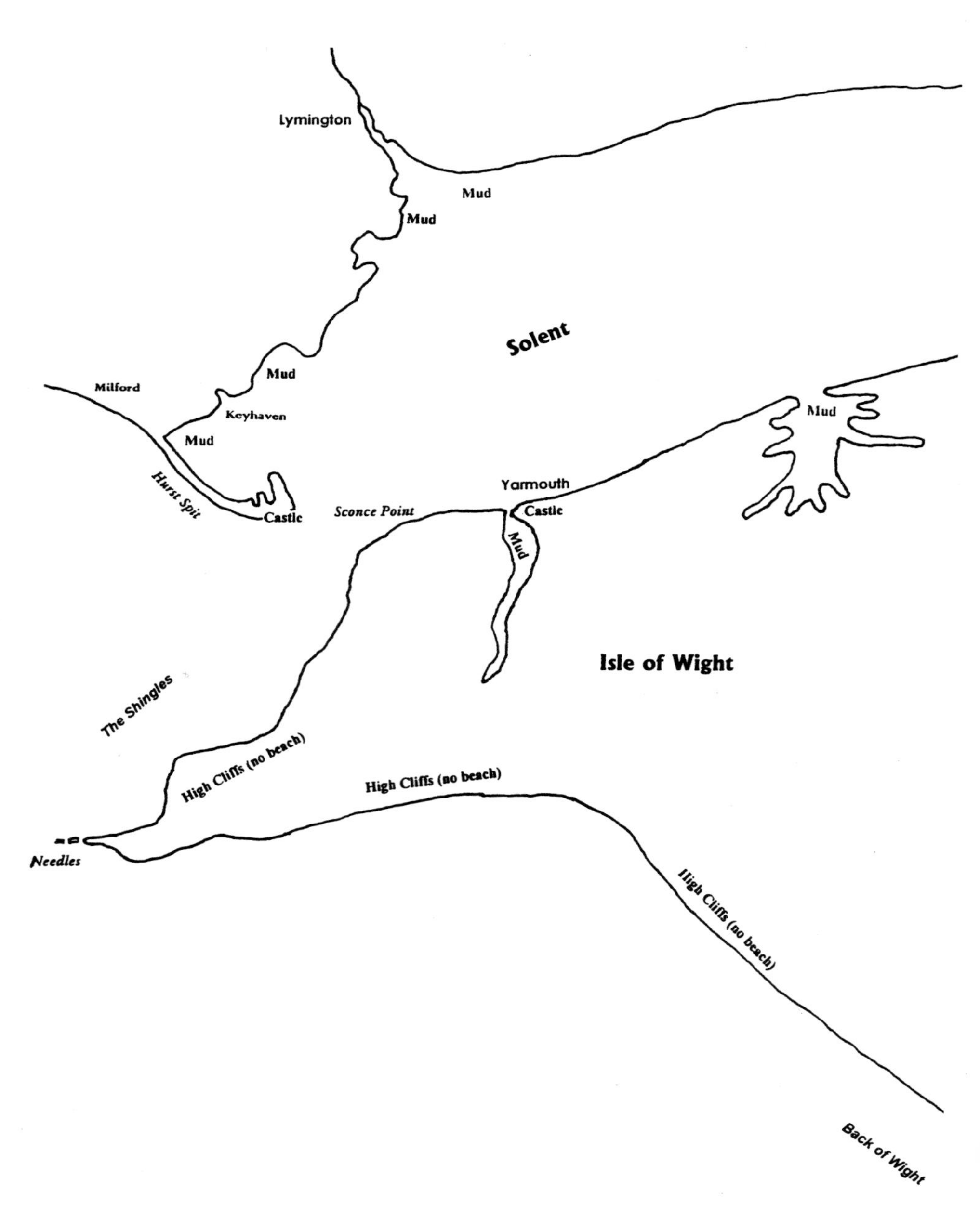

3. Hurst Spit and The Needles

M